"Unless suffering is the direct and immediate object of life, our existence must entirely fail of its aim."

Arthur Schopenhauer

Published by the nonprofit A-Thimbol Inc.

From Creation to Christ

First edition. January, 2024.

Copyright © 2025

All rights reserved. Neither this book, nor any parts within it may be sold or reproduced in any form without permission.

historyreligionandtruth.com

"The simple step of a courageous individual is not to take part in the lie."

Aleksandr Solzhenitsyn.

Table of Contents

1. Introduction: Religion as an Algorithm.................6
2. A Historic Story: Moses and the Exodus............28
3. Once Upon a Time: Reinterpreting Creation......48
4. Adam, Floods, and Exodus: Myths and Realities 58
5. The First Messiah: From Persia to Rome...........70
6. The Christian Era: A Historical Reexamination 89
7. Opinion: The Failures of Christianity...............128
8. Universal Christianity: A New Faith for a New Age...135
9. Platonism to Christianity: The Evolution of Divine Reason...151
10. Kabbalah - Tikkun Olam and the Path Forward 160

1. Introduction: Religion as an Algorithm

Religious narratives have always shaped the way people understand the world. They offer frameworks for morality and purpose, while creation myths give explanations for how existence itself began. However, as our knowledge of reality expands, our ethical frameworks, rooted in faith, must also adapt. Traditional myths must evolve when they become incompatible with contemporary understanding.

By examining history, human nature, and Biblical narratives through a comparative lens, we can trace and analyze the evolving power dynamics from Creation to the first century CE. This analysis reveals how Christianity emerged as a transformative force within the Roman Empire's political framework, and how today, with some modifications to the dogma we could better align the faith to modern intellectual and moral progress.

Through teachings and practices, religions establish moral and ethical frameworks that guide communities, similar to how algorithms define a sequence of steps to achieve specific goals. Religion serves as a cohesive force that shapes our culture. This underscores the significant influence of religious systems on social dynamics and their pivotal role in molding the nature and quality of civilizations.

Recognizing religion as an algorithmic construct provides a framework for understanding its impact on communal behavior, cultural norms, and the overarching character of societies.

Societal behavior reflects the collective beliefs of its individuals, with religion serving as a primary vehicle for imparting our shared values. Many individuals will adopt inherited beliefs without critical examination, then defend them passionately regardless of their truth or logic.

Mimetics is the study of how ideas and behaviors replicate through imitation, the theory reveals how societal norms propagate regardless of personal belief systems. Even non-religious individuals internalize thought patterns from dominant religious frameworks in their culture. This innate tendency toward social mimicry often supersedes critical analysis, causing individuals to emotionally defend ideologies with fervor despite logical inconsistencies.

Belief systems, more than personal understanding, often dictate societal norms. This dynamic makes populations susceptible to manipulation, a tactic well understood and exploited by those in power throughout history. Religion, as a cultural institution, has frequently been employed as a tool to shape and control collective thought.

We are more affected by what others believe than by our own independent search for understanding.

Since religion shapes the people who surround us, and in turn they shape us, we must make certain that religion be truthful as well as beneficial. By fostering an open source environment where questioning established dogmas is encouraged, religious institutions can evolve into centers of inquiry and enlightenment, promoting a more functional and progressive society.

If a society malfunctions, if we see injustice, it is because the algorithm, or the religion and beliefs of society are faulty. If we want a good life, to live within a society that is not dysfunctional, we must modify the religion of the land until it provides the desired effect.

In scrutinizing the Western Judaeo-Christian-Islamic religious model, one observes a potent algorithm that has for nearly two millennia, empowered a ruling class while subjugating a peasant class. Based on superstition, this model fosters notions of racial superiority, subjugates women, and discriminates against the uninitiated. Rooted in the Jewish Old Testament, which recounts a history of conflict and promotes the idea of a "chosen people" destined for global supremacy, this framework has historically fueled prejudice, subjugation, war, and colonialism.

Christians regard the Old and New Testaments as a cohesive whole, yet significant contradictions challenge this perspective.

For instance, the Old Testament often emphasizes justice as retribution, such as 'an eye for an eye,' while the New Testament promotes forgiveness and turning the other cheek. These differences highlight that theological and moral frameworks evolve, and must continue to change as we evolve. One of these important contradictions is in Corinthians where it says that The Old Testament, creator God, has blinded people from the truth of the true God. The Old Testament God is seen as malicious, and akin to the Platonic Demiurge, Great Architect, or Satan figure, thereby designating the "chosen people," as chosen by a false god - or Satan.

The Epistle contains a theologically problematic assertion: *"The god of this world has blinded the minds of the unbelievers"* (2 Cor 4:4). This passage, has distinct Gnostic overtones, introduces a cosmological dualism that fundamentally contradicts the uncompromising monotheism of the Hebrew Bible (e.g., Isaiah 45:5-6). The retention of these contradictions within canonical scripture suggests not an oversight, but a deliberate dialectical strategy.

Historical analysis reveals that this theological ambiguity served a critical socio-political function. The synthesis of Hebrew scriptures with the Pauline corpus created a dual-natured religious framework:

1. A Pacifist Ethos for the Governed
The New Testament's injunctions to non-resistance (Matthew 5:39), love of enemies (Luke 6:27), and exaltation of the meek

(Matthew 5:5) functioned as an effective mechanism for social control, encouraging subservience among lay adherents.

2. A Militant Framework for Rulers

Concurrently, the preservation of Old Testament narratives celebrating divine-sanctioned violence (e.g., Deuteronomy 20:16-17, Joshua 6:21) maintained a theological basis for institutional power and martial authority when required by temporal needs.

This structural contradiction resulted in a system which enabled ecclesiastical authorities to retain institutions of harsh tyrannical power in the face of the Christian Logos.

People will rationalize contradictory doctrines rather than abandon deeply held beliefs. Thus, the "god of this world" reference remains both canonical and largely unexamined, its Gnostic implications neutralized through institutional interpretation. What appears as theological inconsistency may be a sophisticated mechanism of social control, one that has maintained Christian viability across two millennia of radically changing political landscapes. The implications for studies of religion and power dynamics are profound.

This has been our algorithm or set of instructions and has been responsible for the nature and behavior of Western civilization, it has both ruled us, and failed us for many years.

Of course, if you believe that a master-slave society is a good thing, then this religion has been ideal.

I believe that philosophy and science have moved ahead, while religion is dogmatic and changes slowly, that we have been left with a belief that is better suited for the middle ages, and is no longer appropriate for our current society.

In the 19th century we began to recognize that our belief had become inadequate, as was notably pointed out by Friedrich Nietzsche.

"God is dead. God remains dead. And we have killed him. How shall we, murderers of all murderers, console ourselves?"

Nietzsche speaks to the fact that the "Age of Enlightenment" began an erosion of our belief, and that society's view of the existence of God had become unreasonable. The old dogma had been proven false, and now found itself unable to stand against modern thought.

Nietzsche does not indicate that religion is no longer needed, quite the contrary, religion is what gives society stability. He suggests a new dogma based on our "will to power," for power is what will fulfill the "will." This is a dogma for those superior individuals, who are above the law, for those who rule, those who he calls "Supermen." To Nietzsche, Christianity is a dogma for the meek, and a belief designed for enslavement, an ideology which is destructive to his "Superman." Nietzsche sees Christianity and its moral laws, as what is given to that part of our society which serves the Super-class of men who rule. He has simply re-stated the justice of the strong,

Machiavellian political theory, a concept of justice for those who know the path forward, and make it their will at any cost, certainly not how the "Equal Justice" of a Democracy should work.

"I love him who labors and invents, that he may build the house for the Superman, and prepare for him earth, animal, and plant: for thus seeks he his own down-going." — Friedrich Nietzsche, Thus Spoke Zarathustra

Nietzsche's suggestion is quite functional, and works well as long as the lower class does not get wise and revolt. This only gives us the Old Testament law without God, and the glorification of the master slave paradigm. It does have an enormous, obvious, and yet a mostly unmentioned flaw.

What is the purpose of any human "will to power"?

What is the point of having a "Will" if it is only to have power over others? For that matter, what is the ultimate point of any activity which the "will" pushes us to do, and are we not by the motive of this "will" actually deterministic automatons? Since no one has ever given us a fundamental reason for our actions, or purpose for existence itself, it is simply absurdity to go off doing anything without knowing "why" in the first place.

Without a defined purpose for existence how can the "will" be defined? For that matter, how can God be defined without a concrete basis for existence.

When Maxwell discovered electromagnetism, someone asked what the purpose of his discovery was, he answered, "what is the purpose of a new born baby." No known religion or philosophy provides a realistic answer to the purpose of existence. If a "Superman" is expected to act, it would be prudent to first know why, and what verifiable purpose this "Superman" may have to exist at all.

I will suggest a religion that actually makes sense of why we're here, something that doesn't feel absurd. From that, or from another good explanation, we could come up with a new set of guidelines to help us live together more peacefully and in harmony. We need both rules of conduct, and a premise for existence, along with an honest position or perspective of the unknown, or metaphysical. A truthful basis for theology and its rules would then need to stand up to critical scrutiny, not as we have now, a dogma accepted only by faith.

EVOLUTION

I've lived for 70 years, and the only consistent meaning I've found in life is evolution. Primarily ones personal evolution from childhood to adulthood, and if fortunate, into the wisdom that comes with old age. It also encompasses cultural evolution, from the Stone Age to our modern society. While some may seek different sources of meaning, the concept of evolution provides a broad framework for understanding our place in reality. I view life as an evolutionary journey that demands constant learning and growth. However, this perspective may not satisfy everyone, as most prefer to find meaning through faith and an afterlife tied to biblical dogma.

The Bible offers meaning but can also mislead. Faith is necessary because we know so little and often rely on belief rather than facts. As for the afterlife, I see it as an excuse for avoiding the hard work of truly examining life and living as we're meant to.

When dissatisfied with life, we instinctively long for heavenly solutions. However, if religion gave us the right guidance, we would find fulfillment in what we've already been given by God. The fault isn't with God, but with us.

Nonetheless, even without having a meaning for life, each individual lives and identifies with his community. If religious, he is given and accepts some sort of faith based explanation for creation, powers of good and evil, along with laws or rules of conduct to live by. The individual, completely unaware, will then participate in deterministic behavior based on a belief which is derived from the social norm of the community, and period they belong to.

"The morality of the individual, then, consists in his fulfilling the duties of his social position". General Introduction to the Philosophy of History, G.W.F. Hegel

An even deeper connection between the society we inhabit and individual behavior can be found in the work of anthropologist René Girard. Girard proposed that human desire is not an individual projection onto objects but rather arises from the imitation of collective or social influences, a phenomenon he termed *mimetic desire*. This theory, which has gained increasing recognition in recent years, is now supported by neurological evidence and aligns with what social scientists refer to as *group intelligence*. These insights reveal that our social behaviors have deep and ancient evolutionary roots, tracing back to our pre-human origins.

The process of humanity, and the inevitable future evolution of civilization is mostly unaffected by individual belief since each individual is directed not by himself, but by the causal effects of the social construct it lives within. Each of us is a unit tied to a social order, we become who we are due to the period and location we live within. Our social order includes parents, family, language and nation, and we are deterministic creatures that do not deviate from our trajectory.

For example if an individual has concepts and beliefs which are outside of the social norm, society will push against this individual to either isolate them, or to eliminate the belief.

Religion is that social construct, even if it is an atheistic political ideology it is the causal environment that gives form to individual actions. In a sense we are in a box, a deterministic construct, where the outcome of behavior is predetermined by religion and community. We change or evolve only when outliers envision new norms from outside of this box. Then, we can change what we teach ourselves, what we believe will change, the community will evolve, and thereby affect the quality of life.

Social behavior cannot change without altering a community's foundational beliefs, as individuals seeking change are often pressured to conform to societal norms. Since religion underpins community beliefs, only a new religious framework can effectively drive lasting transformation.

God is how we define unknown metaphysical and incomprehensible physical terms like "the infinite." Human evolution creates new technologies, we expand reality, the more we learn and create, the greater the complexity we generate, and the less we can comprehend of the vast expanse of the reality that unfolds before us. While scientific advancements may have challenged traditional explanations of God, the role of religion in shaping meaningful beliefs about the unknown and the causal remains more vital than ever. If Re-Legion is the way we tie society into a pre-described social construct, it would be wise to reconstruct a new belief that is not dedicated to enslavement, discrimination, or untrue explanations of reality. We require a belief that is truthful, one that can say when something is unknown, and not simply make things up.

When I first came across Friedrich Nietzsche, my takeaway was not religion. It was his concept of eternal recurrence, as explained to me in a book called, The Physics of Immortality by Frank Tipler. This is the idea that in an infinite universe, made of finite matter, any state, entity or events will repeat eternally. A human life within such an eternal universe will recur indefinitely, a virtual proof of eternal life. I would then discover that the eternal recurrence was a flawed concept. For me this came from understanding that the universe is not eternal, instead, it both expands into a distance we can not see, and draws into black holes. The universe, as we know it, will go away, thus potentially making any moment unique and unrepeatable. Of course, if there are infinite universes we will re-live our lives an infinite amount of times, and in infinite varieties, but this is immaterial to our particular reality, and would only make our reality even more unique and significant to us.

Religion can be truthful, scientific, and equitable. As an example let us consider the promise of eternal life. If we had the right technology maybe life could be eternal, at least for our intent and purpose, and there are ways of explaining eternal recurrence within a finite universe. Yet, the current theological promise of eternal life is malicious, as you would go mad if you were forced to live forever. On the other hand each life is mathematically equally significant in the structure of space-time, you can not remove a single beggar, nor is a genius more significant than a fly. Although difficult to grasp, even small changes accumulate into profound effects over time. Each life leaves a lasting imprint on the unfolding of events, shaping the future in ways that endure beyond our awareness. In this sense, life is eternal.

Unfortunately, most religions replace fact with faith, science is dismissed, and we lie to our children to enforce false beliefs.

Religion has never been about truth, it is instead an algorithm for power through the subjugation of a peasant class. The Latin phrase "In hoc signo vinces," is conventionally translated into English as "In this sign thou shalt conquer," this phrase is the sign of conviction given to us by the Roman Emperor Constantine, that Christianity would be the religion of conquest and domination for the West.

The realization that western religion was in fact malicious is what shifted my interest from physics, to religion.

MY SENSE OF GOD

I grew up Catholic, but not religious. When I was young I enjoyed studying, and wanted to know a reason for life, and a cause for suffering. I had built a website for personal use, as a tool to help me study. The technology permitted me to copy, paste, and catalog information. My primary interest was in the study of entropy. I wanted to know why life was an ordered complexity, that came from a process we understood as chaotic. An evolutionary process that over time provided us the reality we see and live today.

At about the age of 50, I concluded that the physical universe was deterministic. That the chaotic physical nature behind the ordered structure we apprehend, only appears chaotic due to our inability to do the math of complexity. What we perceived as chaos was an inability to comprehend large infinite sets, and the breakdown of the differential equations we use to define the complexity of physical reality.

Metaphysics will always be with us because there are limits to math and logic. We observe reality in terms of the future, past, and present. In a similar manner to how we forecast the weather, we have only a probabilistic view of reality because the equations required to truly understand the future and past are too large for us to solve, they can only give us probabilities. There is a limit to our logic, to our thinking, just as we can not ask a dog to understand calculus, we can not go beyond certain limits of understanding. This is why metaphysics, and an accompanying religion to explain the unknown, will always be with us.

My conclusion was that there was a definite order to chaos which we were not designed to comprehend. Reality is not chaotic or random but an ordered evolving super-deterministic system. Chaos only appears chaotic to us because our math is incomplete, and therefore we are unable to see order when measuring the complexity that underlies reality. The physical reality we live in is deterministic, which indicates that the future is as immovable as the past.

The non-determinism of quantum mechanics is sometimes proposed as a potential physical mechanism for free will, suggesting nature itself is not causally predetermined. This is because the role of the 'observer' is misunderstood, which in quantum theory refers not to a conscious mind but to a physical measurement interaction.

Founders of quantum mechanics, like Max Planck and Erwin Schrödinger were deeply uncomfortable with this non-determinism. Planck, a determinist, believed a 'conscious and intelligent Mind' was the ultimate matrix of all matter and that quantum indeterminacy would eventually be explained by a more complete, deterministic theory. Similarly, Schrödinger believed the probabilistic wave function was an incomplete description of reality and sought a return to deterministic physics.

Their hopes for a local deterministic universe were largely ruled out by Bell's theorem and subsequent experiments. These experiments demonstrated that the predictions of quantum mechanics are correct and that the universe cannot be both local and deterministic. This leaves us with a choice between a probabilistic reality, and non-local deterministic theories.

If we accept non-local deterministic theories, such as the pilot-wave theory or de Broglie–Bohm theory, then reality is deterministic. These interpretations of quantum mechanics propose particles will always have definite positions and their trajectories are guided by a universal, non-local wave function. The theory is deterministic because the future of the system is fully determined by the initial state, but it is non-local because the wave function's influence on a particle is not limited by distance, connecting distant particles and allowing for "spooky action at a distance" to be explained physically.

Physics is not the point of this book, yet our lack of free will is an important aspect of how I believe faith must be structured, in addition the non local aspects of determinism point to a universal God.

For me, the only possibility for "free will" is through what we define as the grace of God. God became real to me, not by faith, but in fact.

> *There can be only one substance, God , and*
> *everything else is merely a mode of God.*
> *Baruch Spinoza*

The following two facts supported my belief:

First: Religion, and our belief in God, is the algorithm that shapes our society, and builds our future. Although God can be denied, it can not be denied that people believe in God, and that our belief in God has been responsible for the shape of human cultural evolution. God is the unknown causal factor of the Alpha and Omega, the incalculable stream of creation. Reality is an evolving system which increases in complexity with the passage of time, who's underlying causality is the unknowable God. Evolution is an increasing complexity and means the unknown is increasing in scope. Since technically the unknown will continue to become greater, it can not be denied that there will always be a need for metaphysics to make sense of the unknowable.

The realm of what can not be known must be given words and form, thus we will always need some form of faith to give meaning to the unknowable, call it God, or first cause, or any other term we wish to call that which we do not understand, that which is the underlying cause of human behavior, civilization, and reality.

Second: In a finite deterministic universe, entropy is the motive force for human behavior and its civilization. This is the force that will obligate an evolution far beyond our limited human capacity to participate or understand. We must recognize that we are a limited subset of a much larger reality which is constantly evolving and increasing in complexity.

Life is an emergent layer of the physical universe, intelligence is an emergent layer of life, and civilization is an emergent layer of intelligence.

What we call life or reality has evolved for billions of years, and has increased in complexity over time. It is therefore only a matter of time before the increase in complexity will effectively make any imagined ideals real, making each of us an integral subset of a single universal reality with a range we can call Alpha to Omega. Christianity would say a subset of Christ, for we are not eternal, and God is the true Alpha and Omega.

"I am the Alpha and the Omega, the first and the last, the beginning and the end." Revelation 22:13

We have limited motivations and desires, we create surplus, and we can build any Utopian concept we may have imagined or attributed to our prophetic past, present, or future concepts of God.

Although God is unknowable, we tend to think we know God

and must consider that any God we can imagine may become a reality.

It is without doubt that there will be a revelation, and ideals conjured or desired will be fulfilled. Even if we may never know God, the prophecy we choose will become our reality. This future reality we build is of course dependent on our choice of prophecy, and it is this choice which is most crucial to our social reality.

Currently we are still mostly stupid hairless apes, with very poor manners. Therefore the version of Utopia we create may well be dystopian. This is why it is critical that we be truthful and educated enough, to care for and educate, not only our own kin, but everyone else that lives on our planet, otherwise fools will build hell, and we will live there.

We should note these wise words from the past,

"There is only one good, knowledge, and one evil, ignorance." Socrates.

A proper education is the solution to our dilemma, therefore, we must provide a proper education for every living soul. Because we live on one planet, and are social animals who suffer due to our surroundings, our well being is dependent on the quality of the education our neighbor was provided.

"...whatever you did for one of the least of these brothers and sisters of mine, you did for me." Matthew 25:40

It is absurd to have a society as we do today with an ignorant servant class providing leisure and wealth to an upper class of pointless ignorant consumers, all in an eternal struggle for sexual dominance.

Religion must go further than just words and belief, it must actually take responsibility for the physical reality we live. Much too often priests washed their hands of the responsibility for the immoral, ruthless, corrupt, and unscrupulous aspects of society. "The devil did it" is an unacceptable excuse, the fact is that, "we did it," and religion must be held responsible for our acts. Religion can not just be a structure for belief, and ideology for the worship of God, but must also tend to the governance of the economy and community it ministers to.

Our priests and ministers must stop being complicit with the nobility which profit from war, or subjugate their congregations. The accepting of blood money at the offering plate must stop, and change into a process which builds an economy where the Church is a transparent financial institution operated by its parishioners, for the benefit of all. If the "chosen people" are to be our priest's then this concept must be theirs to produce and administer, assisted by Christians and Muslims. Since Judaism has become Kabbalistic and the Kabbalah is Platonic, and Platonism is Christianity, then we could all agree to repair the world, what Jews call TIKKUN OLAM.
A DETERMINISTIC UNIVERSE

The Western concept of God has evolved over time, and eventually a final and more truthful concept of God will emerge as we continue to evolve intellectually. This final concept of God will integrate our past history and traditions with science pointing to a final stage of evolution, and prescribe existence in a new and emergent future for mankind. Thus making our concept of God seamless with reason, logic, history, reality, and time.

I say a final version of God because we are humans, we may extend our lifespan, but our brain is finite. As animals, our language and experience has a limited number of variables. Although we are complex, the variables that motivate us are finite, our desires or "will" is finite. If we eat too much chocolate we hate it, too much complexity bothers us, there is a finite set of variables in an equation that when solved, will make us happy. Happiness in fact has minimal needs, and is attainable for everyone.

Because of the finite nature of our minds there is a limit to what we can understand, and this final version of God will attend to that limit. Since besides knowledge, all we really want is to be happy, there is an equation for that, which is: the minimization of desire and the satisfaction of what remains.

Since we live in a deterministic universe, the future and the past have specific relation to each other and are of the same substance. For this reason any concepts of God are rooted and implicit in both the past, present, and future. Our Judaeo-Christian God is a historical representation of the past, present, and future, with a Utopian view of salvation from suffering at some future point. I suggest that today, that now is that future point.

We falsely see ourselves as having free will, with desire, or a "will" acting within, and somehow separate from our universe. Arthur Schopenhauer, in The World as Will and Representation, explains that life has a "will" which motivates our actions, the metaphysical and the physical reality are intellectual representations we develop. It is this representation that defines what we call conscious and collective consciousness. God is a representation we develop of the metaphysical that drives physical reality and defines our place with the deity. Who would disagree that our concept of God, or the interpretation of creation and existence we have is the product of the universe, of God. Since most all science points to a deterministic universe, then what but God could be pulling our strings. What we call our "will," or that which Hegel calls "spirit" is as deterministic as a canon ball.

A deterministic universe says that God is the basis of all. Moses, Christ, Buddha, Mohamed, etc… are all part of how we try to understand God. Reality is complex, we tend to imagine what we do not comprehend, plus the chaotic incomprehensible nature of entropy makes all reality rooted in metaphysics, so regardless of how scientific or pragmatic we hope to be, the understanding each of us may have of reality is in fact, faith based.

Since I came from a Christian background, when prompted by my new understanding of reality, I began to look into Christianity for an explanation of God. After an initial study I had a born again moment, then after further study I discovered contradictions. A dissatisfaction arose in me which led to a more truthful representation and belief in God.

This essay is the deconstruction of western religion as contrasted with history and human nature. Conclusions are then drawn as to the functions of religion in society, and a new direction is suggested for moving forward.

God can be seen in history through the contemplation of the events between the unknown creation and expiration of our universe. If we believe in one, Universal God, then everything that we see, all reality, is from God.

Therefore history would be the permanent record of the intentions of God, fulfilled.

Before I tell my short story of history, may I say that if you are curious about God, know that good and evil are not aspects of the almighty. Although very much a part of Christian dogma, it is inappropriate to see God as dualistic, manifested by a conflict between divine forces, as in, good God versus an evil Satan. We should know there is only one God, and it is unknowable.

For as I passed along and observed the objects of your worship, I found also an altar with this inscription: 'To the unknown god.' What therefore you worship as unknown, this I proclaim to you. Acts 17:23

Evil is described by Socrates as the outcome of our ignorance and stupidity. Evil is a word we use to describe a value we give to a point of view. Consider a fox eating a rabbit, the rabbit may sense evil, while the fox sees only the satisfaction of dinner. If evil is what torments us, the recognition that evil is only a point of view, that what is evil for me is satisfaction to another, this simple and innate truth should put an end to evil for good. It would then be honest to say the truth will set you free (of evil), simply be smart enough not to become what is for dinner, and don't eat your brother. Still, if you find you did eat your brother, don't ever say the devil made you do it, simply accept you're an idiot, and don't repeat the act.

This exploration will challenge traditional constructs, offering critical insights into their limitations and highlighting the need for a re-imagined framework for faith that better serves humanity's intellectual and ethical evolution.

2. A Historic Story: Moses and the Exodus

When we study history, we should be skeptical and assume that many events are fabrications, and best understood in probabilistic terms. It is essential to approach ancient narratives with a healthy skepticism.

Many events recorded in religious texts may be embellished or entirely fictional, reflecting the cultural and moral values of their time rather than literal truth. For instance, many scholars today regard Moses as a mythical figure, an archetype rather than a historical person. The stories attributed to him in the Torah likely served as tools to unify a people and convey deeper moral or spiritual lessons.

History is the story we tell ourselves, it shapes our identity and informs our understanding of who we are. Yet, can we truly claim that history is anything more than a constructed narrative? Much like our vision of the future, history is often shaped by subjective perspectives and selective storytelling. Just as we use reason to anticipate what might happen tomorrow, we should apply the same critical reasoning to interpret the past. By examining history through the lens of human motivations and power dynamics, we can see it as an account crafted to serve those in authority, rather than as an absolute truth. Only by verifying the facts and reconstructing history in a more reasonable light can we approach a deeper understanding of the past.

This historical account begins by exploring the parallels between the creation narratives in Egyptian mythology and the Book of Genesis. It then reinterprets the Biblical figure of Moses in the context of the Hurrian or Hyksos exodus, ultimately suggesting a connection between Jewish and Egyptian systems of governance.

Through the Babylonian, Persian, Greek, and then finally the Roman conquest of the Jewish people, the common Hebrew is governed through an aristocracy, who in turn are at the service of the empire of the day. It would be significant to understand that today this aristocratic form of governance has not changed, although we pretend a democracy and equality of citizenry.

This will be a brief historical outline which will extend from the edges of prehistory into the first century. A connection between history and religion will be presented that will show many events in a new light, considering religion as a necessary and common tool for manipulating people.

I hope to present a cause-and-effect scenario of history, to demonstrate the effects religion has had on civilization, and finally I will describe a different belief which may work better.

To get a proper sense of the historic period that gave us our religion we should see humanity and its civilization as an entropic machine that is sustained by fresh water. I say entropic because all life functions by taking energy from the entropy the universe produces, humanity and the civilizations we produce are chemical reactions, all be it very complex. Look at our civilization more as you would see a chemical experiment, as deterministic given the elements and conditions of the reaction. Take into account that all of civilization is but a brief moment in the context of the universe, that the reaction we have seen these past few thousand years is almost insignificant in the expanse of time.

According to the anthropic principle, the universe by its nature admits the existence of intelligent observers within it at some stage of its development. The chemistry that underlies the evolution which produces intelligence and then a civilization is entropic. The concepts of entropy and thermodynamics are fundamental to physics and underpin biology, particularly in energy transfer and the organization of living systems within the context of the Second Law of Thermodynamics, which states that entropy (disorder) always increases in a closed system; therefore, living organisms must constantly expend energy to maintain their ordered state.

The Nobel-laureate physicist Erwin Schrödinger stated in his 1944 book *What is Life?* that life feeds on negative entropy, or free energy, eating, drinking, breathing and (in the case of plants) assimilating. Life evolves in complexity which is demonstrated in the distinction between the vast complexity of a single human being to the far greater organizational complexity of a civilization.

> *The general struggle for existence of animate beings is not a struggle for raw materials – these, for organisms, are air, water and soil, all abundantly available – nor for energy which exists in plenty in any body in the form of heat, but a struggle for [negative] entropy, which becomes available through the transition of energy from the hot sun to the cold earth.   Ludwig Boltzmann, 1974*

If I may add to what Boltzmann said: air, water and soil, are not all abundantly available, water for human evolution must be fresh water and is only found in wells and rivers. Therefor if you wish for a civilization to prosper you will need a large river.

As today we fight religious wars over oil resources, in the times of Moses, water was the contested resource. True power came not from the people that lived in the region, but rather the waters of principal rivers like the Nile and Tigris-Euphrates that provided for them, for you cannot have a civilization without fresh water.

At the geographic center between the Nile and Euphrates are the people of Canaan. This region stands as the gateway to the economic power and wealth of the Nile River, the object of conquest from before the time of Moses to after that of Jesus Christ. All armies attempting to control the Nile would need to cross through Canaan and its inhabitants.

Instead of a well-intended concept for saving an enslaved people, you may consider the story of the Exodus as a brilliant plan to protect the Egyptian state. How could we overlook the benefit of moving a population, or just using the preexisting inhabitants, then instilling in them a religious requirement to defend their land, and of all lands, Canaan.

MOSES

It is certainly a possibility that this promised land was promised by an Egyptian Pharaoh-God, in order to put in place a people to defend against invaders from the east, a people destined to be the gatekeepers of Egypt. A land populated by devout believers, charged with protecting a territory given to them by God. This would surely make them the most dedicated defenders of it. We certainly defend property with more vigor when we think it's ours, and even more so if we believe God has given it to us. You may also consider today's war in Palestine as no different, a people put in place in the precise location, to control the surrounding nations which may oppose the West. Who funds Israel? ... little has changed.

Recent archaeological understanding reveals that the area of Canaan was populated by modest people with a Temple that would be destroyed or built by the dominant invading force of the time. No palaces or homes for an aristocratic class. Canaan was a land inhabited by people with simple yet comfortable lives, as those that would be afforded to military families. Contrast this to all the lavish tombs and temples found throughout its neighbor Egypt.

Today we find a similar development in Israel, populated by people who have one of the best military forces in the world.

Given this perspective, we will consider the Jewish war history up to and during the time of Jesus Christ.

By the time of Christ, Rome had put an end to the Pharaohs, destroyed the Jewish temple and made Egypt the personal property of Augustus Caesar. The greatest revolt against Rome is by the Jews, not only in Palestine or Canaan, but throughout the Roman empire. The historical account of these wars, must be seen as a struggle for dominance within a changing world political landscape.

Although presented as a messianic movement, this conflict must have had economic backing and what better source could there have been than the disenfranchised rulers of Egypt and its Greek counterparts. We tend to leave out the larger fact, that it's not only the Jews that have been conquered by Augustus but the entire Hellenistic realm, the Egyptians, Persians and Greeks have now come under Roman rule.

We will look into Rome's attempt to stop and then adopt this Christian political movement. From the family of the Julian rulers to the takeover in 69 A.D. by the Flavians under Vespasian, and then onto Titus. Vespasian will end the reign of the Julian Caesars and see an opportunity in adapting the Christian message to the further benefit of his authority. Finally, the firm establishment of Christianity in 325 A.D. by the Neo-Flavian, Flavius Valerius Constantinus.

This paper and project looks at Christianity, and Judaism in the context of our modern social order, using what evidence can be found to best define a Christianity which has defined Western Civilization these past 2000 years.

We know that it was not until the protestant reformation that we were permitted to read the Bible in our own language. We discover the New Testament is a revolutionary document which calls for the abolition of the Jewish-Roman government, foments individual personal authority, and calls for a new world order. It is understandable that the authorities and its Church would not want its people looking closely at the details of this message. There is good reason for rulers to keep the Bible, and much of history away from the eyes of the commoners who serve them.

Yet, the calming aspects of Christianity, its nonviolent selfless humility and love of neighbor are aspects that serve the more violent dominant supermen of our upper classes very well. How well would it work to be a dominant superman without the multitudes of meek to till the earth.

"There is no God, but don't tell that to my servant, lest he murder me at night." — Voltaire.

History is written by the victor and information is power. Ignorance is not bliss, but a prelude to servitude. Reasonable minds would think that changes in the dogma would have been directed by those in power. A story created as the essential rule set to provide for a well-behaved population in service to a nobility. A carefully designed algorithm for a desired social outcome.

The force that dominates and motivates us all, is what is responsible for the religious algorithm we currently operate from. From what German philosophers call "the will to life", we developed our mistaken relation to God.

This innate set of desires, "our collective will," is no different than those of any primate. For this reason, the biblical story we gave ourselves is no more than the projection of our natural behavior of sexual competition, the same motivation that causes the behavior of all primates and has motivated evolution from single cell life forms to modern civilization. We made a story that reflects the nature of sexual dominance that propels evolution, the desire of one troop of apes to dominate over the other, and then told a story within a theological format.

If we contrast the Biblical account against our human nature, then add to this new archaeological and historical evidence, we will see a long sad story of war and enslavement that still persists today. We can then take a sober view of religion and build a new foundation for belief.

The resulting perspective could lead us to a belief that is more realistic and practical, a belief that is based on logic and reason. A revised Christianity which is truthful, placing the cause of suffering on human shoulders, and eliminating any spiritual aspects of good and evil. Evil or suffering must not be seen as caused by divine or metaphysical forces, but as an aspect and component in the sexual competition of evolution. Suffering is the result of ignorance, greed, and the multitude of sins that would not be so if we only educated our kin properly.

Since religion has been a creation manipulated by the political necessities of the domestication of a servant or slave class, we should take the statement "the truth will set you free" to heart. We must restructure and construct a religion based on an algorithm that is designed to improve the quality of life, rather than one which promotes superstition, serves power and enslaves others.

One of the principal points of this argument is that indeed the Bible has been tweaked over time by the self-interest of Egyptian, Persian, Greek, and later by Rome to serve the Roman aristocratic class, molded into the ideal tool for dominion.

The purpose of this book and website is to place historical events in logical order, and then provide a guide to anyone that is perplexed by the absurdity that is discovered when comparing science, archaeology, and history to the Judaeo-Christian story. I hope to encourage the development of a more adequate story we can tell ourselves about who we are, and better define what our purpose for existence may be.

> *"So that, now as formerly, religious doctrine, accepted on trust and supported by external pressure, thaws away gradually under the influence of knowledge and experience of life which conflict with it, and a man very often lives on, imagining that he still holds intact the religious doctrine imparted to him in childhood..."*
> *Leo Tolstoy*

WHEN WAS YEAR ONE?

Beyond the Gospel accounts and a disputed passage in Josephus, there is little contemporary history of Jesus. If the

Gospels were written to advance a Christian message, then it is the message itself, not precise dates or the literal accuracy of events, that would have been important. In the absence of evidence, it is difficult to insist that Jesus was born in the year one, or that he lived exactly as described in the texts.

Today, theologians have built a hypothetical collection of primary Jesus' sayings they call the Q Gospel. Q may have been the original Christ from which all the other Gospels come from, which would have been dated prior to what we understand to be the life of Christ. The idea of the Q Gospel presents the possibility that there was an unknown individual that existed prior to what we today consider to be Christ.

Nonetheless, for anyone living today Jesus Christ was the most important event of those years, as the account has transformed Western Civilization for these past two millennia. Yet, when compared to the other events that occurred at the time of Christ your perspective may change.

If there is no record of the precise date of the birth of Jesus Christ, how did we come to this date for our calendar?

For me, it is most likely that it comes from the Cult of Mithra, a secretive group of men who studied astrology, understood the procession of the equinox, and decided that the new age of Pisces had begun with the reign of Augustus Caesar. An Astrological determination by a Zoroastrian cult, represented at the birth of Christ by the Three Wise Men, or Magi.

For the uninitiated, and later codified by the Church, we have the common understanding that it is the birth of Christ.

Before I detail the history behind this date, let me explain how power has always been held in secret.

That rather than dismiss conspiracy as a fringe eccentricity, we should recognize it as a pervasive and enduring element of the human social fabric, as hardwired into the architecture of human history and society

Power, in its essence, is not merely a commodity to be possessed but a dynamic and relational phenomenon and its most potent expression is always, ultimately, over others. It operates through the control of narrative and the shaping of perception, but its foundation is the creation and maintenance of asymmetry: the subjugation of another's will to one's own. This is why secrecy and conspiracy are its supreme instruments; they are the means by which subjugation operates without the consent of the enslaved, manipulating the realities that govern behavior while ensuring that the mechanisms of control remain hidden, and thus unchallenged. Its ultimate expression is not brute force, but the silent, uncontested orchestration of a field where the subjugated still believe they are free.

Ideally, power is best served by the construct of complete social illusion, whereby the individual acts in concert with the will of power without being aware of the overarching conspiracy. This is the essence of the Jesuits' 'Third Sacrifice,' a profound spiritual and psychological doctrine.

The 'First Sacrifice' is the surrender of one's material possessions. The 'Second Sacrifice' is the surrender of one's own will and judgment to that of religious superiors. But the

'Third Sacrifice' is the most complete and insidious: it is the surrender of one's own intellect and perception of reality. It is the internalization of the institution's will to such a degree that the individual no longer experiences it as an external command, but as their own most deeply held conviction and desire. They become a self-guiding instrument of power, freely choosing the path that has been laid for them, believing it to be the product of their own free will and rational mind. In this state, the conspiracy is complete not because it is hidden, but because it has been made invisible, it operates through the individual's own consciousness, making the illusion of choice the most perfect mechanism of control imaginable.

Although most people remain unaware of it, this is the foundation of Guy Debord's Society of the Spectacle. Power manufactures the Spectacle, and we, often without realizing it, become its followers, surrendering both our intellect and our perception of reality to a carefully constructed illusion. We are all in a sense victims of Stockholm Syndrome at the hands of our captors. The line in the poem by Alfred, Lord Tennyson. "into the valley of death rode the 600," can be symbolic for all of us, it is to our Spectacle we owe our allegiance, a Spectacle of family, church, football and country all carefully crafted by well organized and hidden power structures.

This is why understanding history, and the very reason we have a 'Year One,' requires us to see power as the art of crafting an illusion. This illusion sets a stage upon which the common man willingly walks the path to his own servitude. And because this grand performance must be concealed to remain effective, the existence of servitude will always necessitate the hidden architects of secret societies.

Year one marks the beginning of our Western Spectacle: a carefully orchestrated stream of consciousness that we still follow today.

The clearest Biblical account says Christ was 30 years old at the time of his baptism, in the fifteenth year of the reign of Claudius, (Tiberius Claudius Caesar Augustus Germanicus).

"In the fifteenth year of the reign of Tiberius Caesar, Pontius Pilate being governor of Judea, and Herod being tetrarch of Galilee, and his brother Philip tetrarch of the region of Ituraea and Trachonitis, and Lysanias tetrarch of Abilene, during the high priesthood of Annas and Caiaphas, the word of God came to John the son of Zechariah in the wilderness. And he went into all the region around the Jordan, proclaiming a baptism of repentance for the forgiveness of sins... Now Jesus himself was about thirty years old when he began his ministry. He was the son, so it was thought, of Joseph, " (Luke 3:1–23)

The following is the best reference for why our calendar starts as it does.

This dating system was created by Dionysius Exiguus in 525 A.D., who lived in Rome and wrote guides on Church administration, and mathematical works. Dionysius chose to start the new calendar with the year he believed to be the year of Jesus' birth, which he calculated based on various historical sources available to him at the time. He arrived at the year 1 AD as the year of Jesus' birth, although modern scholars generally believe that Jesus was born a few years earlier, between 6 and 4 BC. He lived 200 years after Constantine's Council of Nicaea and only 95 years after Rome had been sacked by the Visigoths (410 A.D.).

The Latin term Anno Domini (A.D.) translates to "Anno" as year, and "Domini" which was the title given to the deified Roman Emperors. For the Emperor as the Lord of his people, has dominion over them. For the Romans as for most civilizations, religion and its priest class is the political means of popular dominion, and Rome sees its emperors as Gods. For anyone living anywhere in the empire, after year one, Augustus Caesar is the undisputed Lord God, whereas Jesus Christ is mostly unknown.

The idea of an emperor as a deity would be a whole different world from our current concept, this highlights how deeply the roots of the political-religious structure intertwine.

This dating system was not fully accepted until the 1400's. Spain and Portugal continued to date by the Era of the Caesars or Spanish Era, which began counting from 38 BC. In 1422, Portugal became the last Catholic country to adopt the Anno Domini system. It is believed that the Spanish Era was set up by Caesar Augustus when he first levied a general tax and mapped the Roman world in 38 BC.

In any case both calendars were based on a calculation for Easter, relative to a mathematical approximation of the first astronomical full moon, on or after 21 March. Before the Julian calendar, several different calendars were used by various civilizations and cultures around the world.

The Roman calendar was reformed by Julius Caesar in 45 BC. Called the Julian calendar, it is not dependent on the observation of the new moon but is an algorithm which introduces a leap day every four years. The oldest calendar still in use is the Jewish calendar, which has been around since the 9th century BC. It is based on biblical calculations that place the creation at 3761 BC. For the Romans under Augustus Caesar who had control of the known world, it was his calendar the empire would use, and for the Catholics of the 6th century it would be the Anno Domini system.

What we all use today is the Gregorian calendar, a refined Julian calendar which was introduced in 1582, and is the "de facto" calendar for secular purposes. The Gregorian calendar is currently used by most of the world. It was introduced by Pope Gregory XIII in 1582 as a reform of the previous Julian calendar. The Gregorian calendar is a solar calendar that is based on the Earth's orbit around the sun and includes rules for leap years to keep the calendar in alignment with the seasons.

Regardless if the Christian epoch starts in 38 BC or year one as it is today, this will be the start of our Roman era, which began with several very important events that are rarely mentioned in Bible study.

1. 47 BC, a child is born between a Roman God and an Egyptian Goddess, who is later said to be missing or killed.
2. 44 BC Julius Caesar is assassinated and is posthumously granted the title Divus Iulius (the divine/deified Julius) by decree of the Roman Senate on 1 January 42 BC.
3. 32 BC The final battles of a World War are in Israel against the Jews.

4. 30 BC Two divine rulers, Cleopatra commits suicide, and her co-ruler son and Pharaoh Caesarian is presumed dead.
5. 27 BCE The end of the Roman Republic, it was this year that the senate conferred on Octavian the title of Augustus (The "Revered one"). "Divi filius" a Latin phrase meaning "son of god" was a title used by Augustus who was the grand-nephew and adopted son of Julius Caesar.

The Roman God Julius Caesar was assassinated, Cleopatra the Goddess and Queen of Egypt commits suicide, and their 17-year-old son, Caesarian, a Pharaoh is presumed killed.

This young boy was the eldest son of Cleopatra and Julius Caesar and had been declared by Caesar to be the next emperor of Rome. As a child, he was the personification of the God Horus, he ruled Egypt jointly with his mother Cleopatra, from September 2, 44 BC to August, 30 BC. The royal family of Cleopatra would have married with the Jewish Kings to maintain alliances; therefore, this child would also be a descendant of King David. I could imagine that some mystics of those times might consider Cleopatra not only a Macedonian, but also Jewish.

This 17-year-old Pharaoh was allegedly killed by Octavian, who would become the next Roman Emperor, and change his name to Augustus Caesar.

It could be said that the following historical events were triggered by the birth of Caesarean.
—The assassination of his own father Julius Caesar in 44 B.C.
—A Roman civil war that would become a World War stretching from Greece, through the old Persian empire, Egypt,

and ending in Israel.
—The suicide of his own mother, goddess of the Egyptians, and a Greek Macedonian Queen.
– The destruction of the Temple in Jerusalem, and the Jewish dispersal from the promised land.

These very important events would have never occurred, were it not for the birth of this child.

Caesarion is omitted in the religious account we are told, but for the Egyptian cult of Isis and Horus, these events would have been critical. The cult of Isis, continued to be practiced in various parts of the Roman Empire, including Rome itself, well into the 4th century CE and would have been well known to those attending the Council of Nicaea.

The god Horus was often depicted as a child on his mother Isis' lap. Some claim parallels to the virgin birth and resurrection themes of Christianity.

The Madonna and Child (Mary and Jesus) is arguably the most iconic and enduring savior-child narrative in history, deeply embedded in global culture through Christianity. While other myths share motifs, none match its religious centrality, artistic legacy, or worldwide recognition.

So, what happened to this child?

As told by the victors, the Romans who won this world war, this child was killed. Yet, there are accounts that the child was taken to India, as his mother Cleopatra had ordered.

The murder and suicides of these individuals, whom would have been seen as Gods to the people of this era, would certainly have affected things. These events, if included into the Christian message, would have had great significance to the Greek and Egyptian Gnostic people to whom the apostles were evangelizing.

From the supposed death or disappearance of this child in 30 BC to the final battles for Israel in 135 AD, we will see the Jewish Temple destroyed, Israelite's sold into slavery and dispersed throughout the Roman empire, as well as the life of Jesus Christ and his Apostles.

For the people of Israel, these times must have been of Biblical proportions. All major world religions would have seen this as a great message of some sort. The most secretive cults of the Roman Rulers, the Egyptian Priests, Zoroastrian Magi of Persia, Greek Platonists, Druids, the Cynics, Pythagoreans, Stoics and so on… these events would certainly affect all religions of the empire. I would say particularly affected would be the ruling class of Roman Mithridatic cults in Tarsus, from where the Apostle Paul would come from. These Mithridatic cults had many Christian similarities of worship which would later be incorporated into the Catholic Catechism.

The Egyptians had lost their God Pharaoh and would never be re-established… and the Jewish people had lost their Temple and promised land. Certainly, we should mention this history when we discuss Jesus Christ, but strangely we overlook it.

These historical events, when placed in the context of the life and teachings of Jesus Christ, present a different perspective on the history and intent of our religion.

So what reason would there be to omit these historical events from the Christian account?

I would say it is because the Christian account is based on the Old Testament, is historically Jewish and not Roman, and was propagated by Jewish Apostles. Although the Gnostic versions of this salvation story rejected the God of the Old Testament, this would not be the story that would be promoted by Rome. In fact, it was critical for the Roman Church to make this new religion centered on the God of the Jews. Consider this story of Christianity not as isolated to the First Century but as a story that continues up to today. From the act of Flavius Josephus of coming to the side of the new Caesar Vespasian, through the tax collector Matthew and prosecutor Paul, to the Jews who worked as administrators and tax collectors for Polish feudal lords, or Israel today as the military arm of the West.

You may consider the Diaspora as more of a relocation of administrators throughout the empire.

Christianity will make your servants docile, while the "chosen people" administer the realm, all well overseen by the Roman Catholic Priest class.

'History is a set of lies agreed upon' Napoleon Bonaparte (maybe)

If history is a lie, then our history should at least make sense, its parts should fit, in context Caesar should be as important as Christ, a world war should be included, and human motivations for power must be accounted for.

So, let's make up a new story, and to properly tell this story we must start with the creation account of Genesis.

3. Once Upon a Time: Reinterpreting Creation

Egypt was the economic powerhouse of early civilization, and a central player of a biblical account that became the foundation of western religion. When you consider the cultural and economic power of Egypt with its proximity to the promised land, to what extent does the Genesis creation narrative show Egyptian influence, and what is the probability that its core elements were an Egyptian creation?

The origins of biblical monotheism may owe much to a dialogue with both Egyptian and later Persian history. Scholars have long drawn parallels between the Exodus narrative and the expulsion of the Hyksos, a Semitic people driven out by Pharaoh Ahmose I in the 16th century BC. Even the name *Moses* has been linked linguistically to the *-mose* found in Egyptian royal names such as *Ahmose*. Later, in the 14th century BC, Pharaoh Akhenaten staged a radical religious revolution by abandoning Egypt's traditional pantheon in favor of the worship of a single supreme deity, the Aten, a synthesis of Amun-Ra. His bold monotheistic turn, though short-lived, stands as a striking historical precedent for the biblical Exodus narrative, which tradition places in the 13th century BC under Ramses II.

The question of how these events relate to the Bible was already debated in antiquity. The Egyptian historian Manetho, writing in the 3rd century BC, identified the expelled Hyksos as invaders and then rulers of Northern Egypt, who were later expelled to Canaan. Centuries later, the Jewish historian Josephus expanded on this account, suggesting that the Hyksos "built a city… and called it Jerusalem."

From a political perspective, the value of a unifying religion cannot be overstated. For a new kingdom rising in the contested highlands of Canaan, a frontier zone between Egypt and Mesopotamia, the creation of a national faith centered on a powerful, warrior god served as both shield and rallying cry. A divine mandate, framed as a "promised land," fostered a strong collective identity, justified both conquest and defense, and bound scattered tribes into a single nation. Devotion to a god who demanded exclusive loyalty produced a highly motivated people, willing to fight for territory they believed was granted by divine right. That this land also held immense strategic importance to Egypt only underscores the political dimensions of the faith.

In this light, the God of Israel can be seen not as a simple borrowing from earlier traditions, but as the outcome of a complex matrix of statecraft, shaped not only by Egypt, but also by Persia, and eventually by every empire drawn to the wealth and strategic power of the Nile and its surrounding lands.

When we add this background to the history of the Isrealites, the "One God" people of Moses, the Bible and the Jewish religion have the potential of being an Egyptian and later Persian fabrication.

"Thou shalt have no other gods before Me" is one of the Ten Commandments found in the Hebrew Bible at Exodus 20:2 and Deuteronomy 5:6. The central tenet of the Abrahamic religions is the commandment against worshiping any gods other than the Lord. At roughly the same time, the Egyptians themselves were experimenting with the notion of a single supreme deity. Yet the phrasing of the commandment is telling: it does not deny the existence of other gods but insists upon exclusive loyalty to one. This God demands absolute allegiance, not because rivals were unimagined, but because they were very much believed in. So, who is this God that is to be singled out for the people of Israel?

If I am saying that religion is an algorithm that produces behavior, then the question of what God is that of the Old Testament can be seen in the behavior of its people.

In any society ruled by an authoritarian regime, such as ancient Egypt, the legitimization of the supreme ruler's authority is paramount. The Book of Genesis reinforces this dynamic by presenting disobedience as humanity's original sin, thereby establishing obedience as a foundational virtue. For a servant, the gravest transgression is defiance. Consequently, a religion structured within a master-slave framework must cultivate absolute submission among its adherents, just as in Egypt, where the Pharaoh, as a divine sovereign, demanded unwavering compliance.

In this little creation story of mine... Adam and Eve lived in this perfect land we will call Eden. It was never too cold, plenty of fresh water, with food just waiting to be plucked from the trees. No need for clothes, no need for work, it was a good time until someone eats the wrong fruit.

Adam and Eve will have two sons, Cain and Abel, and Cain will kill Abel. The Cain and Abel account would repeat throughout history. Mankind would continue to kill each other for a variety of reasons, over and over. Nonetheless, the first family grew and multiplied.

Over time many would leave Eden and go east. Those who left would suffer the consequences of leaving Eden. They had to wear clothes to protect themselves from the elements. They made tools to work the land, and would cultivate dominion over the beasts. Life was a bit more difficult for them, but what does not kill you makes you stronger, so they prospered.

They worked in communities, and could talk to each other. They stood upright on two legs. They could out run all the other beasts, and could travel to far off places.

They were the cleverest of all the creatures on earth. They built communities of individuals, with a variety of personalities. The curious ones looked at the stars and would learn when to expect the seasons. These would become the wise men, the priests, who would keep their knowledge secret and pass it on from generation to generation.

They discovered that knowing when the seasons would come was valuable. With their knowledge, they could better provide for and defend the community. They would gain the trust of the people. These early mathematicians and astronomers would create our first religions, and will use religion to govern these early societies.

The difference between slave and master is culturally defined from the intrinsic "will" of a primates biology. The dominant male ape becomes the Pharaoh, and civilization will consist of tyrants that will control a community made of others enslaved who serve them.

Let us not forget that these are primates that lived in Eden, and would remain primates as they populate the world. What I am describing is the creation of our human civilization, which is simply how primates behave when they can talk to each other. No amount of education, or modernization can erase the intrinsic will and nature of the animal we are. Unless we first recognize our true nature which lies in the motivation that produces behavior, both individual and social behavior will be determined by our basic animal motivation, that which is sexual dominance.

Sexual dominance is ingrained in our ape DNA, and this motivates evolution and determines the nature of human civilization. More aggressive individuals will always enslave the quiet, polite, and meek. **Only if we evolve away from sex driven social behavior will the absurdity end.** The meek will not inherit the earth until our competitive nature is modified, only then might we have the compassion required to actually produce equal justice.

Over time an aristocratic ruling class would grow along with the size of the community. In time the educated aristocracy would become God-like to all the others, and all would look to them for protection.

In the first 100 thousand years of human life, we had learned how to read the stars, and predict the seasons to plant our crops. The aristocracy had learned that they could create a "reality" for the people that served them.

Just as animals could be domesticated, they would domesticate people, and slavery would become a normal part of life.

You see, even though we know we come from something in the past, we can only remember the past we have personally lived. When each of us is born we start afresh... we have no idea who we are or where we came from. You can tell us any past, or reality you wish and we will believe that reality.

Rulers had discovered that the history or religion they told their subjects would create their reality. A population could be given any story and it would become true. Lies would become the truth, and then defended by the very people you have lied to. Imagine that your parents never told you Santa Claus was not true, and made certain you were always fooled. Just like children we want to keep believing.

May I repeat this quote,

"History is a set of lies that people have agreed upon,"
Napoleon Bonaparte (maybe)

Religion is a standard history you give to everyone in the realm, a story that unifies the community to its ruler. The Egyptian priest class were experts in eternal life, let's say... If you are a good Egyptian, the Priests can offer you eternal life.

For Judaism it was a covenant from God, a chosen people and a promised land. For the Persians it was a struggle between good and evil and the eventual salvation and victory of the good God Ahura Mazda.

In the first century, for the Roman empire and its newly conquered Greek states the appropriate religion will be Christianity. Christians will get a combination of all the religions of the newly conquered Roman empire by Caesar, the Roman "Son of God," Pontifex Maximus, Caesar Divi Filius Augustus. Christianity would not come from Augustus, nor any of the subsequent Julian family Caesars, but rather the clever successor of Nero, Vespasian who established the Flavian dynasty in 69 AD.

The Christian Logos incorporates its Trinity and Soul from the Greek Platonists, eternal life from the Egyptians, the struggle of good and evil along with Satan and an apocalyptic end times from Zoroastrian Persia, and finally central to the religion will be the Messianic call from the Jewish Torah. Christians will get forgiveness from sin, and salvation as long as they accept Christ, and the Logos as written.

I am getting ahead of myself, I will return to the start of civilization and the purpose of religion… those that knew this trick would be the most powerful of all, they would become the priest class. These priests would hold the truth of the past secret, and would keep it to themselves. They would create a fitting illusion of reality for the others, a reality tailored to make them willing servants. Entire civilizations could be put in their hands. They would keep civilizations in an illusion. Like Plato explains in his allegory of the cave, we become so trusted in our illusion that we would kill anyone that would bring us the truth.

The ruling class would be very cautious as to whom they would share knowledge with. They created elaborate initiations, with stages to go through to test if applicants were trusted to keep secrets, and worthy of truth and knowledge. That's why, "the truth will set you free".

Ten thousand years ago, the people of the land of Eden were the Egyptians, and their river was the Nile. Further east of Eden would be the Sumerians, and Babylonians of the Tigris and Euphrates rivers. To the North, nothing but barbarians. We make the mistake of overlooking the North when we consider early civilization, but those Barbarians must not be left out, for they will become the ultimate rulers, the true chosen people.

A calendar of the cosmos would be deciphered. Gods would be seen as the celestial bodies, becoming the central hallmark of all early civilizations. They studied and interpreted the universe and its God-Stars, which they believed controlled their reality.

The Chinese, the Indians of India, and the Indians of America, no matter where these wise men would go they would take their knowledge, given to them by their forefathers. They would govern their people as slaves and their people would love them as Gods. They would prosper from the ignorance of others. They knew they only had this power because of the ignorance of their subjects, therefore they must enforce ignorance. Secret societies and mystery religions would become the norm.

Most archaeologists say humans came out of Africa. Rivers are the easiest way to travel, especially if you go downstream. The most powerful early civilization was from the river where all humans had come, the Nile, in Egypt, they were the Egyptian Pharaohs. The High Priest-Pharaoh would be created in the image of his particular reality. This reality would then be given to the slaves, they would live and worship the Pharaohs reality. Time would begin with the Pharaohs' reign. Then the slaves would be told of the fantastic mythical and heroic deeds of the Pharaoh. The slaves would love the greatness of the Pharaoh, and call him God. They would till the soil for him, and would fight battles against other rulers from far off lands.

To the Egyptians order was life, and chaos was what opposed life, they were who dictated the order on earth. They believed the greatest and most heroic of them were the personification of order, and must surely be touched by the Gods. Given the time and place, all this would make perfect sense to these people, great men would of course be seen as Gods. Even today, it's not difficult to feel superior when you are better educated, have more money, or power, you tend to see yourself as a superior breed. Then as today, power tends to make us think that all the other people on earth are here to serve us.

As great civilizations arose, their leaders would see themselves as the central cause of their civilization. Their domination of others, would of course, be the proof of their divinity. They were the closest to God, sons of God, maybe heroes of virgin birth, or engendered by Gods that would come from above to have their way with beautiful women. Fantastic accounts would reinforce the notion that God had put all the other people on earth to serve them.

This will be the standard by which the world works, until the time of the Greeks and their short lived Democracy.

We don't know why, but around 500 BC, throughout the world there was a radical new change in thinking. In Greece the pre-socratics created philosophy, and the first ideas for a democracy began. Confucius in China teaches kindness and equality to others, and places family above the state, and the Buddha will teach moderation and asceticism to India.

A transition in thought is occurring, yet will never really take hold. Advocates of freedom and justice like Jesus Christ, and Socrates are killed. The old primitive primate code of justice never changes. Justice is to be loyal and defend your allies, your troop, nation, or clan, all while harming all others. This is the code that will produce tyrants and empires... for empire after empire!

This barbaric notion of justice has remained, the divine right of kings is still something we contemplate, and little girls are still taught to want to marry a prince.

The entire methodology behind modern government stems from evolutionary conditions. All language, history and theology is constructed from basic animal desires, motivation, and behavior. The dominant ape was once called the Pharaoh and has evolved into the concept of Pope or President. The names may change but the "will" that makes us behave as we do has remained unchanged.

The truth is something very few people concern themselves with, only a minority care for anything beyond the quality of eating, shelter, and sex. Leaders have no incentive to provide higher education to a slave class, so the unfortunate aspects of slavery still persist although under the illusion of freedom.

The truth will transform our society. If Socrates said, "the un-examined mind is not worth living," then would not the same apply to the un-examined society. All our problems rest on the fact that we are more concerned about what is for dinner, than why we eat and exist in the first place, and if we do wonder about our existence we have a religion that tells us a lie.

As I hope you know by now, I wrote this history because I believe we are currently positioned to truly step into a new society, and have developed a method for open direct democracy. If we use the internet and social media for targeted education, and we manage our economy as an open transparent direct democracy, we will eliminate the need for an alpha male, and tyrants will be no more. We could then actually live within a society that provides equal justice for all, a reality similar to what we have only imagined as utopia.

4. Adam, Floods, and Exodus: Myths and Realities

After a period of 100 thousand years of steady cooling, the temperature of earth begins to rise.

There is a theory called the Younger Dryas impact hypothesis, which contends that an extraterrestrial object exploded over North America around 11 thousand years ago, initiating the Younger Dryas cold event, the extinction of many North American mega-fauna, and the demise of the Clovis archaeological culture.

The warmer and wetter climate in the Southern Hemisphere helped human migration into South America. At the same time the populations of the European Northern Hemisphere were forced into southern migrations.

Around the same time, about 10 thousand years ago, there was also rapid warming, populations increased, and a property of evolution we call civilization emerged. Around 6000 to 5000 BC, the Mesopotamian and Egyptian civilizations began to develop.

Migration and trade between northern European tribes along eastern trade routes will stimulate interactions with the settled populations of Mesopotamia. As trade increases, northern traders will begin to threaten the wealthy established southern civilizations of Egypt, Babylon, Persia, and Carthage. About 2500 years ago, barbarians from the north began to conquer and absorb these civilizations.

Perhaps these migrations came with different mindsets. Living in a harsh northern climate, with a different diet, may have made these people tougher and more serious adversaries. Cold weather does have a culling effect on the weak. In addition, unlike the cake eaters of the south, the northern Europeans would have had a diet consisting of more meat. Not only would the additional protein make for larger people, but it also helps in brain development.

In my lifetime archaeologists uncovered Göbekli Tepe. This is a Neolithic site in the Southeastern Anatolia Region of Turkey, which existed between 9500 and 8000 BC. This predates most Egyptian and Mesopotamian civilization, and indicates to me that these northern hunter gatherers were not as barbarian as we may think.

I consider Macedonia, Assyria, and Greece as cultures that are strongly influenced by northern tribes. From about 1200 BC till the final conquest of the southern civilizations by Alexander the Great in 320 BC, we see a steady attack on southern civilizations by northern Europeans.

These northern tribes would confederate and influence Mediterranean civilizations. Possibly as soldiers with the sea peoples which plunder Egypt, as well as the Greek/Macedonians that will ultimately conquer Egypt and Persia.

ADAM AND EVE

Before the wars of northern aggression began, the civilizations of Babylon and Egypt had become the great civilizations we know today. Between Babylon and Egypt we see the struggle of Cain and Abel, an ongoing account of one killing the other, with Israel in the middle. In fact all history has been made of one civilization trying to kill the other.

The influence Egyptians had on the Israelites, must have been significant. With the exception of Moses' account of an

Exodus, and the Merneptah Stele, history as well as the Bible tells us that these two people lived in relative peace and next to each other for thousands of years. With no mountains to separate them, no walls, we see no fortifications built between these two peoples.

If you look at this in terms of human dynamics, you will see the resources of the Nile river and its civilization as a prize to be taken. Any band of tough guys would have seen the advantage of taking from Egypt all they could. We also know that the Egyptians were powerful and clever, they were more than capable of conceiving ways to protect themselves.

The story of Adam and Eve, and the history of Abraham is told by Moses to the Israelites. In this historical account of the Jews, we come to a time when the Jews were slaves in Egypt. Moses is planning to have them escape from the richest land in the world, to be relocated to exactly where all enemies of Egypt will need to come through to take the Nile river valley and its resources. But, before this can happen, a back story is given called Genesis.

The creation story of the Israelites is very similar to the Egyptian creation story. In the Egyptian story, God comes from chaos and creates the earth, the sky, the night and the animals. The Egyptian story has Osiris and Isis instead of Adam and Eve, Osiris is killed by his brother Set. Whereas the biblical creation account has Cain killing his brother Abel. In addition, Cain the bad son heads to the East.

This would work nicely if you wanted to have these people distrust anyone coming from the east, for they are the sons of

Cain. Especially effective if all your enemies are from the east, like the Babylonians and Assyrians.

The Egyptian belief is that the first population of earth are Gods, but in Genesis they are humans. In the Egyptian story God created the heavens and the earth, but heaven and earth are understood as Gods. In one Egyptian myth, humans are believed to have been created by the gods to serve them and to maintain order (maat) in the world. Humans were seen as a crucial part of the divine plan and were expected to fulfill their roles by living virtuous lives and upholding maat.

In the Genesis 1 account, God created the heavens, the earth, and man and woman in his image. Then by the seventh day it is done. But wait, he actually is not done, he has forgotten something, In Genesis 2, as an afterthought a working class is created for he forgot there was no one to do the work.

"And every plant of the field before it was in the earth, and every herb of the field before it grew: for the LORD God had not caused it to rain upon the earth, and there was not a man to till the ground" Genesis 2:5

God now creates Adam and Eve to till the earth and work the garden. I would suppose Adam and Eve are made to serve the Man and Woman earlier created in God's image during the first seven days of creation. Obviously if you are made in God's image you don't till the earth, that's what slaves are for.

The parallels between the Egyptian religion and the old testament are quite numerous, to the extent of archaeologists finding Biblical verses in Egyptian literature such as the Instruction of Amenemope.

The main takeaway from these stories is that they are myths, designed to govern people through superstition. In the Biblical Genesis, we not only see similarities with the Egyptian account, but the groundwork for establishing a slave class and positioning the Jewish people as warriors and servants of God, a narrative that laid the foundation for the tragic course of Western history.

THE FLOODS

The Ice Ages began 2.4 million years ago and lasted until 11,500 years ago. The world would warm up, and if our concept of God is the Alpha and Omega, then climate is an act of God, and for this account, this is when God created man. Current evidence suggests that modern Homo sapiens appeared in Africa around 190,000 BC, so we were around far before 11,000 years ago, but we began to act like the humans we know today around 11,000 years ago.

As ice began to melt, the seas and rivers would swell, and great floods would come. It would stand to reason that as most people lived along the rivers and seas, catastrophic floods would have been an increasing problem for them.

The peoples of the northern lands would have found their lands more plentiful. With shorter winters and longer growing seasons, populations would grow in these northern regions and they will do what all humans do, breed, overpopulate, and migrate.

As harsh conditions change into the relatively warm and calm forests we now know of Europe and Western Asia, populations develop into new civilizations, and begin to trade with the northern outskirts of the established Egyptian and Babylonian civilizations.

An emergent property of life is civilization, and this was starting to emerge 6000 years before Christ, and its character was shaped by floods and migrations. Current archaeological finds may indicate that religion, and civilization began not in Egypt, but in Macedonia and Turkey. Exactly in the region where the northern migrations and trade routes intersect with the southern middle eastern people.

Hunter gatherers move with herds of animals, and migration expands cultural experience. In a sense the sons of Cain who left Eden, in Africa, 100,000 years earlier, would travel the earth and eventually return.

A journey of thousands of years was now in this man's collective memory. These people are coming out of the woods, their theology is evolving from animal Gods, to conceptual Gods of the human condition. It is striking that many still resist the idea of evolution, even as we continue to evolve in how we understand God.

In the ancient world, war gods such as the Greek Ares or the Roman Mars commanded devotion, for war was central to survival and identity. The divine realm, the Pleroma, teemed with gods, and people chose their deities according to their needs, sailors turned to Poseidon, farmers to Demeter, soldiers to Ares. The Hebrew tradition followed this pattern: Abraham names his God first *El Olam*, then *El Shaddai*, and Moses later calls him *Yahweh*. Whatever the name, the God of Abraham emerges from a context of violence, leading a band of mercenaries, and bears the mark of a war god. Only later does this God come to be seen as the one God above all others. Yet the Bible itself speaks not of one but of many gods, while demanding absolute loyalty to this one above the rest.

As human understanding evolved, prophets and rulers began to declare the supremacy of a single god. In Babylon, Abraham rejects the gods of his homeland in favor of one sovereign deity. In Egypt, Pharaoh Akhenaten elevates the Aten above all others, abolishing the old pantheon. In Persia, the Zoroastrians proclaim Ahura Mazda as the supreme God. In each case, the choice of god reflects the character and needs of the people who venerate Him.

Mount Ararat is where Noah is said to have landed the Ark, and is located in Eastern Anatolia, a region of modern Turkey. The people that lived near Mount Ararat were the Assyrians and will later be called Persians. They will in time become believers of the one God Ahura Mazda (Ahura - lord, Mazda- wisdom), and their prophet is Zarathustra. The Assyrians are from the same region of the Hyksos, who will later become the Israelites.

Abraham comes from the city of Ur, in Babylon, and will become the patriarch of the Hebrew people. Abraham will travel from Ur, through Assyrian on his way to Egypt, and from Egypt his people will create the nation of Israel.

The Bible tells us that Abraham lived ten generations after the flood. Abraham journeyed from Babylon through the lands of the Hurrians, Hyksos, and Mitanni, eventually reaching Egypt, where the story begins. The Hurrians and Mitanni, descendants of Noah, shared a connection with Abraham, who worshiped YHWH. The Mitanni, through which Abraham's tribe passed through, became Zoroastrians, worshiping their own single god, Ahura Mazda.

In Egypt the sons of Abraham will meet the illusionists and masters of the Kingdom of Egypt. The line of wise men known as the Pharaohs now come face to face with their past, those that had gone east of Eden have returned. The religion of Abraham, intersects with the religion of the Egyptians. The sons of Abraham who have a covenant with God, one God above all others, will come to eventually teach the great Egyptians.

The character of civilization is built on migrations, people exchange concepts and technologies, and this changes the nature of culture.

EXODUS

Archaeologists tell us that around 3500 years ago (1650-1550 BC) Semitic people from the lands east of Egypt settled in the lands of the Nile Delta. These people are generally believed to be called the Hyksos, a people which may have originated from a variety of regions, including the Near East, Canaan, and Mitanni. The Mitanni kingdom, was located in what is now northern Mesopotamia and Syria, it was a powerful state during the second millennium BC, and had close ties with Egypt through trade and diplomacy. I would suggest since Mitanni had close relations with Egypt at this time in history, the tribe of Abraham, a confederation of mercenaries, would be the ideal source for these people, The Old Testament does tell us that

Abraham and his men traveled from Ur in Babylon, then through Mitanni and Canaan prior to entering Egypt.

Also Moses after fleeing Egypt, following the killing of an Egyptian, found refuge in Midian, a region geographically close to the Mitanni territory, where he married the daughter of a Midianite priest named Jethro, essentially becoming part of the Midianite community for a period of time.

Ancient Egyptian texts, such as the Execration Texts and the Amarna Letters, mention the presence of foreign populations in the Nile Delta region. The Egyptians call these people the Hyksos, or "the foreign rulers," who were defeated and expelled from Egypt in the 18th Dynasty by the Pharaoh Ahmose. The "Storm or Tempest Stela," is a monument erected by Ahmose at the Temple of Karnak, it describes a great storm that destroyed the Hyksos army as they attempted to flee Egypt, which Ahmose interpreted as a sign of divine favor. The Egyptian historian Manetho, who wrote in the 3rd century BCE. tells us that the Hyksos or Shepherd kings invaded Egypt from the east, overrunning the land, burning the cities and destroying their temples, and recounts how the Hyksos were eventually expelled from Egypt by the pharaohs of the New Kingdom.

Then there is the account of the Jewish first century historian Josephus, of which the Jewish Virtual Library says:

> *Josephus identified the Hyksos as the patriarchal Jews, equating their appearance in Egypt with the Joseph story in Genesis and their subsequent expulsion with the biblical tale of Exodus.*

I think we can safely say the Egyptians did remove these people from Egypt, but history can not clearly say where they went.

The Hyksos had infected the land of the Pharaohs with foreign beliefs, such that one of its Pharaohs, Amenhotep IV (1351–1334 BC), tries to convert the Egyptian religion and all its Priests to the belief in one God, Aten.

There are no other archaeological or historical events that parallel the biblical events of the people of Abraham and the Exodus like this one. Carl Jung and Joseph Campbell both believed that the reign of Amenhotep IV, was the most likely time for the Exodus story.

Remember these Egyptian Pharaohs are the greatest of all masters, they have for thousands of years perfected the control of how reality is perceived by their slaves. As today, as well as in the world of ancient Egypt, reality, religion, and history is invented for the working slave class through propaganda, for the benefit of the ruling class.

Keep in mind that in these times, the ruling class believed they were Gods, only a select few could read, and most all people were slaves.

Is the following story a possibility?

The Pharaoh hires a fella called "Moses" to remove the Hyksos from his land and most cleverly places them back to where they came from, next to Egypt and in Canaan. To do this he will give them a new and extraordinary reality. These people, these mercenaries who believe in one God, the sons of

Abraham, they that have infected the land of the Pharaohs, will be given a makeover of biblical proportions.

Thousands are sent into the desert, led by Moses and his priests. For 40 years they are forced to wander in this desert. They walk in circles and starve. A most remarkable form of brainwashing and mind control will occur, mass Stockholm syndrome for a new nation. A generation passes, and a new history complete with laws and commandments is given to them to be believed. They are then resettled at the very border of Egypt, to be governed by Kings they believe to be their own and told that they have been given this land by God. They will protect this land unlike any slave, for they believe they are free, and have been divinely given this land. The truth will be kept from them and they will fight all invaders that come for the rich lands of the Nile.

A short side note: Why didn't anyone ask… "why did the Pharaoh not go get his slaves back?" They could have said at some point in the hundreds of years, "We can't let Moses get away with that! Let's go get the slaves we lost so many years ago!"

There should be some sort of sentiment there, a few wars at least, but nothing, no problems. Plus, there is no sea between Egypt and Israel. You can walk there, in fact it is a walk on the beach, you can go barefoot if you like.

None the less the Israelites do a lot of fighting, just not against the Egyptians. The Old Testament is a war history of these people.

The biggest question I had was: Why have the children and people of our Western Civilization been told this story as fact ever since a Roman Emperor and Caesar decided to do so in 325 BC?

The answer would be that this is a very effective way to rule over others.

5. The First Messiah: From Persia to Rome

The Battle of Carchemish was fought about 605 BC between the armies of Egypt allied with the army of the former Assyrian Empire against the armies of Babylonia, who were allied with the Medes, Persians, and Scythians. The Babylonian alliance under Nebuchadnezzar II, decisively defeated the Egyptian and Assyrian forces.

The prize is of course Egypt, but it would be difficult to control Egypt with the Israelis having settled in Canaan. As they do today, the Israelite's will fearlessly fight for the land that God has given them.

It would be a simple matter to control the slaves of Egypt, for they know they are slaves, and a change of master would go unnoticed, but the Israelite's believe they are free and will cause rebellions.

Solution: In 586 BC the Israelite priests and royal families were moved to Babylon where an eye could be kept on them.

539 BC, the Persians, conquer Babylon. Under the rule of Cyrus the Great, the Persians have a more tolerant policy toward the Isrealites, and return the Israelites to Canaan. The Persian religion of Zoroaster is also of the one God, Ahura Mazda. The Persians are from the lands and of the civilization of Mitanni, where the Semitic peoples of the Hyskos had come from. The land that is next to Mount Ararat where Noah's ark landed. Where Abraham's people came through on their way to Egypt. Cyrus will rebuild the Jewish Temple, restart the Jewish faith, and is canonized as the first Messiah of Israel. The Persians become the beloved allies of the Israelites and the great Persian empire will now stretch from Africa to India.

The kingdom of Israel was destroyed by the forerunners of the Persians, the Assyrians, in 722 BC. It was at this time that the ten tribes of Israel were lost. Would it not be reasonable that these tribes were not lost but assimilated into the Assyrian Empire. Thus making the two remaining tribes loyal to Egypt, and the 10 lost tribes part of the Assyrian empire. Since the Assyrians were incorporated into the Persian empire the 10 lost tribes would also be incorporated into Persia, of course they would help the land of Judah, and rebuild the faith.

It is now 500 years before Christ. The Persians now rule over Babylon to the south, and Egypt to the west, and they will permit the Israelis to return to their promised land.

In 457 BC according to the Bible, the Persian king sent Ezra to bring the Torah, the five books of the Laws of Moses, to the Jews. Modern scholars have claimed not only that Ezra brought the Torah to Jerusalem, but that he actually wrote it, and in so doing Ezra created Judaism. Without Ezra, they say, Judaism would not exist. Under the Persian rule and patronage of King Artaxerxes, Ezra redefines the Torah with more attention to law, and what appears to be an apocalyptic Zoroastrian bend, Ezra has been called the father of Judaism.

For the Persian King, the Jewish religion was ideal for ruling this territory. The Bible served as a war manual, with spiritual ties to both Egyptian and Persian beliefs. Even the name Israel —Is, Ra, El—echoes the names of Isis, Ra, and Elohim (which is plural). This made it the perfect religion for a people situated between Persia and Egypt. In a way, it was the first "Catholic" or universal religion, as what King Artaxerxes did with Judaism in 457 BC, parallels what Emperor Constantine did with Christianity in 325 AD, the establishment of a universal or catholic faith for the empire. The idea of a state religion wasn't Constantine's invention; religion has long been a powerful tool for governance, though many fail to recognize it.

From a military or diplomatic perspective, with Judea as an ally, Persia can now rule Egypt. The Priests and Kings of the Israelites have lived in Babylonian captivity for over 50 years. In a sense the Kings and priests of the Jews have been liberated by the Persians, and would be grateful. The Israelites will call Cyrus the Great, Messiah, God's anointed one. (Isaiah 45:1)

Those who return to control the land of Israel would remain well connected to the people back in Persia, and to the former Babylon. For the Persians to control the new lands of both Egypt and Babylon the Jews are the perfect answer, they are back doing what they know best, the middlemen, administrators, and protectors between power and servitude.

The king of Persia, Cyrus, is now Israel's first messiah, he sets the stage to rebuild the temple (Ezra 1-6), and places the house of David back in control.

535 -516 BC REBUILDING OF THE TEMPLE

Of course the Greeks and Macedonians, who are the arch enemies of the Persians, hate this.

The Israelites exiled to Babylon were not ordinary captives, they were the intellectual and political elite, likely descendants of Egypt's ruling class, steeped in traditions of power consolidation through narrative control. After five decades in Babylon, they had integrated into its hierarchies. When the opportunity arose, only a fraction (roughly 10%) chose to return, not merely as refugees but as a vanguard seeking to reclaim sovereignty and reimpose their authority over Israel

Pause for a moment and feel the times these were. It is around 500 BC that Rome was founded. Pythagoras is in Egypt learning their mysteries and mathematics. Greece is a people that comes in and out of Persian control. Macedonia, where Alexander the Great will come from, were barbarians, and would have been the troops on the front lines of the Greco-Persian wars. 150 years after Pythagoras, Socrates will come to Greece from Persia to teach, and the Jews have begun to write the Babylonian Talmud.

The known world of this time is tyrannical, everyone is a subject or a slave, only in Greece will a few men have some rudimentary form of democracy. For the rest of the world, to not be a slave meant you were not part of civilization, and your children would starve from time to time. To be a slave meant you would worship your master, and participate in the benefits of the kingdom. People want to be good slaves, this is why Moses has a hard time keeping the Israelites from going back to Egypt.

Few could read, and even less studied anything. Scholars would study only within secret societies. Reading or writing was rare, even Socrates disapproved of writing because it made for poor memory. As today, most people simply believed what they were told, and that is how people were governed, through belief enforced by hunger and ignorance.

History shows us that ancient secret societies and priestly classes were very selective about who they taught. Groups like the Druids, Persian Magi, Pythagoras' followers, and the mystery cults of Dionysus and Mithras didn't share their knowledge freely, they treated wisdom like precious treasure to be protected. While regular people received simplified religious stories, the deeper truths remained locked away in these exclusive clubs. This careful control of information reminds us just how powerful secrecy and deception can be in shaping what people believe and how societies function.

With the Pharisees put in place in Israel, the Persians could now rule Egypt through the Israelites, and now have a military force to protect its economic interests. The slaves in Egypt would be ruled by the priesthood and their Pharaoh, and the Israelites would defend the borders, once again all as it should be.

Remember that all this came about because of climate change. Populations are still growing in the north, people are still migrating south.

At this point in our history, continued population increase will fuel migrations from the North, and the building of city states in Italy and Greece. These migrations will fuel the sociological clash between hunters-gatherers, and established river based civilizations. They would come and live on the fringes... they are Barbarians to the Greeks and the sea people to the Egyptians. The people from the colder North that had migrated south are now building states in the north, in places like Macedonia and Villanova. These areas would be the perfect place for them to settle and trade between the northern settlements and the well established Persian Empire. The climate has warmed, their populations culturally stabilized and began to grow and prosper.

MACEDONIA, THE BARBARIANS

From north of Greece, in Macedonia, would come Alexander the Great. In 325 BC his armies would conquer first Egypt, and then Persia.

In Egypt, Alexander fights in Tyre but is welcomed by the Israelites in Jerusalem. He is told that Daniel's prophecy had told of a mighty Greek king that would subdue and conquer the Persian Empire. Alexander then enters Egypt and is welcomed. He is called the new "master of the Universe" and son of the deity of Amun at the Oracle of Siwa Oasis.

Now why would that be? Why would he fight against Tyre but then be welcomed by the Israelites, and then made God by the Egyptians?

The Phoenician city of Tyre, was founded by and is an ally of Carthage and Persia. The Phoenicians were a loose confederation of sea people that traded throughout the Mediterranean. These were independent states, and would have been the commercial adversary of Egypt, Greece, and Persia.

At this point in history, the Israelites would have been the police or army that is governing Egypt for the Persians, once Tyre was defeated, they would now do the same for the Greeks.

Power is pragmatic, religion is for the masses, religion is a theology manipulated by a priest class in favor of a ruling class.

For the Greeks, the God's and religious traditions of the Egyptians are much more akin to them, than those of the Persians and Israelites. When Alexander enters Egypt he would be seen as a liberator, they would be free of Persian rule. The Egyptian priest class and religion is once again whole, and Alexander will be made a God for the occasion.

From 332 to 30 BC Egypt will be Ptolemaic Egypt, during which time Egypt became a thriving bastion of Hellenistic civilization. Until the time of Christ all the Egyptian Pharaohs will be Macedonian kings. For over 300 years, Egypt's ruling class will be predominantly Greek, culminating with the final Pharaoh, Cleopatra, or more precisely, her son Caesarian, whose fate will intertwine with the narrative of Jesus Christ later on.

Since all people in Egypt at this time are slaves and know only what they are told, things go back to normal. The Egyptian priesthood will support the new Greek-Macedonian rulers, the Kings of Judah will govern their people and profit from them under Greek Macedonian rule, and the Pharisees will continue to reinforce belief to the Israelite's. The Priests of the Pharaoh continue to reinforce belief to their slaves in Egypt. The warrior class of the Hebrew once again live in peace with the slave class of the Egyptians, all under the World rule of the Greeks.

By the first century, Alexandria in Egypt had one of the largest Jewish populations in the world, second only to Jerusalem. Alexandria, was the capital of Egypt and a major center of trade and culture in the ancient world, this large Jewish community was well-integrated into the city's culture and was highly influential, with a thriving intellectual and religious life, including the creation of the Septuagint, the Greek translation of the Hebrew Bible. This diaspora community played a key role in the spread of Jewish thought and Hellenistic culture. The Jews had once again returned to Egypt.

In the second or third centuries BC, Greek and Jewish cultures had blended so deeply that Ezekiel the Tragedian, a Jewish playwright, created a drama inspired by the biblical Exodus of Moses. This play merged the scriptural narrative with elements of Hellenistic tragic theater, specifically tailored to engage an Egyptian audience. Imagine the affront this must have posed to the Egyptians, being presented with a spectacle that cast them as villains and exploiters. Such a provocative narrative would only be acceptable if viewed within the context of a Greek-Israeli alliance, where the religious context of the Jews is seen as beneficial to Egypt.

The Macedonians, the once barbarians have done well for themselves. Greek culture and language will dominate the known world up to the time of Christ.

GREECE AND ROME

Western Civilization is thought to have Greek and Latin origins, yet there may be more Persian in us than we credit. Cyrus the Great rebuilt the Jewish Temple and kick started the Old Testament, the Apocalypse, the battle between Good and Evil were Persian Zoroastrian concepts way before they were Christian. Even the concept of the Germanic people as "The Aryan Race" stems from the pseudo-scientific linguistic and historical connection to Persia. This said, Europe may not have come from Eden as it is more rooted in the Greek and Persian civilizations and their traditions.

Macedonia was a land to the north of Greece and Villanova was a land to the north of Italy. Macedonia would evolve into the Greeks of Alexander the Great, and Villanova would evolve to become the Rome of Julius Caesar.

The real power of Rome would be their Republic, built from the democratic or republican concepts inherited from the Greeks. Their soldier citizens could participate in their government, which is unlike the kingdoms they will defeat, whose armies are mostly composed of paid mercenaries, or slaves.

A sense of freedom is the best incentive for a soldier to fight for their nation state. It was a belief in freedom that formed Israel, the Roman republic, and now is integral to the power of the United States.

From the time of Alexander the Great, till about the year 100 BC the world was divided between the Greeks in the East, the Romans in the Middle, and the Carthaginians to the West.

The slaves in Egypt, just as all slaves, would be controlled through ignorance and propaganda. Each time a new Pharaoh came into power, the slaves would be told of the fantastic miracles performed, and great battles with non-existent people. This was the task of the Priests, they would provide public relations in support of the ruling class, regardless of who they may be. The Persian, Greek, and Egyptian upper classes all would enjoy the fruits of the labor of their slaves.

Since knowledge is power, those who know rule over those that do not know. Slaves will not revolt because the concept is inconceivable, within a properly operated slave culture, the only problems that can arise are ones where one aristocratic family member decides to take power from another.

After the conquest of Egypt by Alexander the Great in 332 BC, the new Egyptian Pharaohs would be Macedonians. Although we call them Greeks, Alexander was a Macedonian, his father had for the most part ended democracy, and did not hold any democratic values, in fact everyone of any authority considered democracy absurd.

The generals who were left behind by Alexander the Great would rule a vast Greek Empire. The slaves of Egypt and

Persia need to know only what they are told. The Israelites need to know only what the Pharisees will tell them. No one but those who rule would need to know the truth about anything.

This is the period within which the civilization in Villanova will be assimilated by the Romans, and Rome will begin to form.

PHILISTINES, PHOENICIANS, AND CARTHAGINIANS

To understand the formation of Rome you must understand the "sea peoples" or Phoenicians. The "sea peoples" is a term used by the Egyptians for a people that have come from the sea to raid Egypt.

The Minoan civilization predates this period, and is sometimes considered Europe's first civilization. Some say this civilization is what is described by the legend of Atlantis, and what would later evolve into the Phoenicians.

The Phoenicians were a loose alliance of maritime cities that traded throughout the Mediterranean. They had made the Mediterranean sea their empire, and were in direct competition with early Rome.

The Phoenician port city of Tyre is located just north of Canaan, and flexed its control of Canaan prior to the Israelite move to the area. The Phoenicians were sea people; they traded with Canaan, their city-state was Tyre, and was central for trading to and from the many port cities of the Mediterranean sea.

The Carthaginians are west of Egypt and controlled lands in north Africa and Spain. These people traded and ruled the coastal areas from well protected port cities throughout the Mediterranean sea.

For any people attempting to dominate the Italian peninsula the Carthaginians would be the principal competition.

The Punic Wars, also called the Carthaginian Wars (264–146 BC), were a series of wars between the Roman Republic and Carthage for control over the Western Mediterranean. Rome will eventually destroy Carthage, as well as take the Mediterranean sea for their own.

The Israelites as well as the Egyptians were land warriors, the Phoenicians on the other hand were sea warriors. The Phoenician port city of Tyre dates back to 2700 BC. Located in what today is southern Lebanon, it is believed that these are the same people that founded Carthage. Carthage and Tyre must have also been associated to the Minoan island states of the Aegean Sea. This would make the Phoenicians a civilization in itself, "sea peoples," maybe connected to the legend of the lost kingdom of Atlantis.

In 332 BC Alexander the Great's conquest of Egypt had its battles in Palestine, and particularly against Tyre, an extremely fortified port city with 150 foot walls. The Roman conquest and consolidation of the Italian peninsula was made possible by the Greek conquest of Tyre, as it would have been a key trading partner of Carthage.

The Carthaginians had control of the western Mediterranean. Once Tyre is taken by Alexander, the Carthaginians will make all efforts to regain the Eastern trading alliances the Greeks have taken from them. Carthage and the Phoenician alliance in the Mediterranean will find itself in conflict with Greek, and then later Roman interests.

At the time of Alexander the Great, the Romans were forming their Republic, battling for control of the city of Rome and eventually the Italian peninsula. They are an association of farmers and traders taking lands for defense and personal gain. Their Republic was composed of individuals who could rise according to their value. Early in Rome's career it took dominion of the Etruscan's to the North, then began to attack their neighbors eventually taking full control of the Italian Peninsula.

Rome will begin to gain possessions in Europe, Macedonia, Persia, defeat the Carthaginians, and finally subdue Egypt and Israel. By the end of the first century CE, Rome will have taken control of most of the territories of the Greek world. Two new Roman religions will come to dominate this new empire, Mithraism and Christianity, which I contend are actually one religion.

This timeline leads us to the Rome of Julius Caesar.

212 BC Syracuse or Sicily, once a Carthaginian stronghold, falls to Rome

197 BC Macedonia, the former home of Alexander the Great, became a Roman province.

190 BC The Greek Seleucid rulers of Persia were defeated by the Romans.

The Carthaginians almost ended Rome. Under Hannibal in about 200 BC they invaded Rome by taking troops and elephants from Spain and coming into Rome from the Alps.

Finally in 146 BC the Romans sacked and completely destroyed the city of Carthage.

This unleashes the Romans onto the rest of the known world, and sets the stage for Christianity, and the future Roman Catholic Church.

By 100 BC, Rome has taken control of more and more of the territory throughout the Mediterranean region, setting the stage for the birth and life of Julius Caesar.

The very battle hardened armies of Rome are running out of lands to conquer, eventually they will have only themselves to fight for control of the known world.

Egypt is a land of slaves which can be easy to conquer, but to control Egypt is a separate issue, for its neighbor Israel, has a population of free people who believe God gave them their land, and they will fight to protect the Greek status quo.

Rome is becoming more powerful than the previous Greek empire, and its problems are now internal. To answer the question of, "who will govern Rome?", a family feud of global proportions will ensue.

As we approach year "one", two Gods Caesar and Cleopatra have either been killed, or committed suicide, Persia, and Egypt, and Judea are in the hands of Rome, and more particularly have become the personal property of Augustus

Caesar, the grand nephew of Julius Caesar, who is also known as Octavian.

JULIUS CAESAR

The world we know today, and the way we understand Christianity strangely pivots on the actions of one man, Julius Caesar..

Rome, having fought their way from Villa Nova 500 years prior and now with an army that stretches from Spain to Persia, will begin to fight among themselves for power.

In 50 BC Julius Caesar was heading to Rome to fight a civil war. His troops come from Gaul, north of Rome, and are a popular representative power base that will come to fight his rival Pompey who represents the established aristocracy who wish to stop the expansion of the republic.

Optimates, led by Pompey... Were dedicated to keeping power in the hands of noble families and wished to limit the republic.

Populares, Led by Julius Caesar... Are a Roman aristocracy that relies on citizen and popular support for political power, the spread of mild democracy, if you will.

As Caesar crosses the Rubicon and enters Rome, Pompey and his armies sail to Epirus. Epirus is where the oldest Hellenic oracle is, where Alexander the Great's mother came from. A region that Aristotle considered to have been the most ancient part of Greece and where the Hellenes originated.

Stop and think about this for one moment. These men have gone to the most holy ground they know to fight the last battle of a long civil war. They are fighting in Greece, the land that gave them their Gods. This would be similar to us fighting a world war in Israel, certainly not inconceivable.

In 48 BC at Epirus, Caesar defeated Pompey. Caesar is now appointed dictator, with Mark Antony as second in command.

Pompey and his remaining forces go to Egypt where there is an ongoing civil war between Cleopatra VII and her brother Ptolemy XIII. Pompey goes to Ptolemy XIII for protection, but is murdered by him instead.

Caesar comes to Egypt to deal with Pompey's remaining forces, and is disgusted by the murder of his rival Pompey. He sides with Cleopatra in a civil war against her brother Ptolemy XIII. Successful, he then installs Cleopatra as Queen, and has a child with her, born in 47 BC, only one year after his battle with Pompey.

Caesar has just defeated his rivals for control of Rome. He has won battles, but has not taken control of the economies that the wealthy families of his political rivals, the Optimates, control. He must pay his soldiers, and keep the economy going. Cleopatra is the wealthiest person in the world, she is the Nile river and the source of grain for his troops. With Cleopatra, Caesar has built favored alliances with both Egypt, Israel and the Greek states of Persia, and developed a policy to unite in peace the known world. This is possibly the most remarkable moment in all of human history, a Roman new world order is envisioned.

With this child and his alliances within the Greek order, Caesar can pay his troops and have greater control over the Greek world. With his new family, this child will become the next ruler of not only Rome but Egypt as well. This will cause the Roman senate to fear this dictator, and seed the end of their Republic.

This family of Cleopatra and Caesar is now the law of two religions, the Roman and the Egyptian, and their child will inherit the known world as a God.

February 15, 44 BC Mark Antony placed a crown on Caesar's head, Caesar was then assassinated on March 15, by a group of senators.

Cleopatra - At the time of the assassination of Julius Caesar, had lived for two years in Rome, from the summer of 46 B.C., with their son Caesareon. They would leave immediately after the death of Caesar for Egypt. In Rome, Mark Antony, Caesar's second in command, will try to restore order. Mark Antony will join forces with Octavian, the adopted son of Caesar, and to seal the bond he will marry Octavian's sister Octavia. The alliance between Octavian and Mark Anthony will not last long.

October of 41 BC Mark Antony meets with Cleopatra in Tarsus, this infamous relationship will eventually bear three children. Cleopatra will have four children, one with Julius Caesar and three more with Mark Antony.

Please note Mark Anthony and Cleopatra are in Tarsus, which is where the Apostle Paul is from, this is a central economic region of the Greek power base, a strong ally of Egypt, and of the Hellenized Jewish people.

September of 40 BC Mark Antony who had married Octavian's sister, left her pregnant and returned to Egypt to get support from Cleopatra in his battle with his brother-in-law, and now adversary Octavian.

This World War is all about something very personal, a sorted family matter in which the richest people in the world, who consider themselves God-like, conspire and kill each other to see who will end up with all the loot.

Capturing Jerusalem in 37 BC, Mark Antony installs Herod as a puppet king of Judea.

In 34 BC, Caesarian, the son of Caesar and Cleopatra, then thirteen years of age, was formally made "King of Kings," by Antony and Cleopatra.

A battle would ensue over these divisions within Rome, in 31 BC, with Cleopatra backing Mark Antony. Mark Antony and Octavian would confront each other in Actium, on the east coast of Greece. The battle is here because these are the front lines between Rome, and what was once the Greek empire. Cleopatra who was in fact a Greek Macedonian Queen would be there in person with Mark Antony. As the battle goes poorly for Antony and Cleopatra, they abandon the battle and sail to Egypt.

August 1, 30 BC, Octavian is in Egypt, and takes the city of Alexandria. Recognizing their defeat, First Mark Antony takes his life, and then Cleopatra commits suicide on August 12, 30 BC.

Some historians will say that she sent her son Caesareon to India via the Red Sea. Octavian would say he had killed him and as they say "there can not be two Caesars"

Years earlier in 63 BC Julius Caesar had been declared "Pontifex Maximus," making him the administrator of Jus Divinum or divine law, for life. It is important to consider that Octavian in 31 BC, following his defeat of Mark Antony and Cleopatra, as the adoptive son of Julius Caesar, assumed the title of Divi Filius (Son of God), and renamed himself to Augustus "first citizen" Caesar. A family that will later be the personification of the divine right of Kings, becoming the title of Kaisers and Czars of our western culture.

Augustus would mark the end of the Roman Republic, and the beginning of the dominance of Rome which will form the western culture we find in Europe and the United States today.

Augustus is not the only individual that will claim Divi Filius or the "Son of a God," title. Jesus Christ becomes a direct challenger to Augustus, for he is also to be called son of God. This all while the actual son of Julius Caesar and Cleopatra - the missing Pharaoh and God, Caesarian, will be forgotten, or assume a new identity.

The Roman Republic will end along with the hopes of the republic. The followers of Julius Caesar who had hoped to establish a union between east and west, have lost their battle. This point is argued in light of the fact that although Julius Caesar became a dictator, his troops, as well as most of the Senate, was loyal to him and expected representation in a new government.

This moment also marks the end of both the Hellenistic(Greek) Age and the Ptolemaic Kingdom of Egypt.

The Pharaoh Gods and the priests of the Egyptians will end, the new order is now Roman, and its divine leader is Augustus Caesar.

These are the political and religious events that bring us Christianity. These foundational events are key to a deeper appreciation of the coming Christ.

If we would like to understand Christianity and today's Church, it would be wise to understand the political reality of the period by carefully looking into these historical events.

6. The Christian Era: A Historical Reexamination

"Then, leaving Cleopatra on the throne of Egypt (a little later she had a son by him whom the Alexandrians called Caesarion), he (Julius Caesar) set out for Syria". - The Parallel Lives by Plutarch published in Vol. VII of the Loeb Classical Library 1919 edition.

Before we continue I think a short recap of the history just before the work and life of Jesus Christ would be helpful.

On January 10, 49 BC, Julius Caesar crossed the Rubicon River leading an army of a popular uprising which would take Rome by force. June 23, 47 BC Caesarion was born, the son of Julius Caesar and Cleopatra. February 44 BC, Julius Caesar was appointed dictator in perpetuity, and was promptly assassinated on the 15th of March 44 BC. After the death of Caesar, a battle for control of the empire culminates with Mark Anthony and Cleopatra combining forces. In 34 BC, Caesarian, the son of Julius Caesar and Cleopatra, then thirteen years of age, was formally made "King of Kings" by Antony and Cleopatra. 32 BC, the Roman Senate declared war against Cleopatra. The battle of Actium is lost in 31 BC, Mark Antony takes his life and then Cleopatra commits suicide on August 12, 30 BC.

As head of the victorious Roman army, and as the adoptive son of Julius Caesar, Octavian will claim the title of Divi Filius (Son of God), and rename himself to Augustus "first citizen" Caesar. Yet, there is left the question, where is the true "Son of God" the legitimate son of Julius Caesar, and Egyptian Pharaoh Cleopatra, the thirteen year old boy Caesarian.

The Egyptian priests and Pharisees of the Israelites have new masters, and they are Roman. The Pharisees will once again serve who is in power. A new religion will be given to the Egyptian slaves as well as to the common Greek and Roman subjects of the empire. The Pharaoh is dead and will not return, Egypt will have a new religion under the new Caesar, Augustus, Pontifex Maximus.

It would be in 12 BC, that Augustus assumed the title *Pontifex Maximus*, the chief high priest of the Roman state religion. By uniting political and religious authority, he set a precedent that future emperors would follow. The office of *Pontifex Maximus* presided over the College of Pontiffs, much as today's Pope leads the College of Cardinals. Thus,

Augustus stood as both *Divi Filius*, "Son of God," and *Pontifex Maximus*, the spiritual head of Rome.

Extraordinary times for the birth of a carpenter that will put into place a belief that will persist for more than 2000 years. A work of words, a Logos that will first oppose Rome, and later be adopted by Rome in 325 AD by Constantine as the new religion of conquest.

THE SON OF TWO GODS

I am not saying that Caesarion was Christ, nor do I think it is important today, but I do think he was important to the people of his time. As he was considered the "Son of God," if you were to create a religion for the Romans of the new empire, a secret attachment to their God Caesar would certainly be useful.

Consider the following...

1. Why would the lost years of Jesus Christ match so well with a Caesarion period of exile. In the time of Christ, people who knew, would have taken notice of those lost years. They would wonder if the missing Caesarion had escaped and not been killed by Rome.

2. For the most part, first century Jews did not use surnames, they were most often known by their name and their father's name. But, for a personage as important as Christ, who was being evangelized to the Roman, Egyptian and Greek world, why no real name? When a name is how you denote who you are, where you come from, and who your family is, you would think someone would attach a surname. You may get away with

believing in Jesus Christ, but it would be a problem if you were to tell people Caesarion or Caesar was still alive. The name Jesus Christ is not how people were named, Jesus is "Yeshua" which translates to English as Joshua, and Christ is a title that signifies savior or redeemer, whereas Caesarion is a nickname for a real name, Ptolemy Caesar Philopator Philometor.

3. The New Testament describes Christ in conflict with the Pharisees. His anger at the temple and his concerns with money and wealth, is a political-economic message. The Pharisees are a problem because they side with the Roman governance of Judea. The message of Jesus can be seen as a political-economic plan to eliminate the power of the Pharisees. For the people of the Eastern Roman Empire whom Paul evangelized to, the Christian message of a 'Lord' superior to Caesar was politically subversive. While not a direct call to arms, this theology challenged the foundation of Roman imperial authority. This perceived threat was realized when Emperor Nero, the last of the Julio-Claudian line, scapegoated Christians as enemies of the state. In a final twist of fate, Nero's death would plunge the empire into civil war, ending his dynasty and transferring power to the Flavian emperors, Vespasian and his son Titus, the very general who had been waging war on Judea, and destroyed their temple in 70 AD.

4. Considering how important the calendar and dates were for the Romans and Egyptians, why so few historical dates.

5. Christ comes to the poor and the disadvantaged. It is the carpenters and fishermen that feed and house the people, this is where the real power of humanity is, in its economic

production. The rich do not produce, they supply nothing, and disproportionately consume. The meek will one day inherit the earth, and the truth is what will set man free. This is the economic, and social lesson which is in the new Christian religion, a beautiful concept that can never be when your "Ekklesia" is a tyranny.

6. The apostle Paul would be able to rally many followers because influential people know the political realities, and understand that religion governs the masses. They may have known Christ as Caesarian, the Pharaoh, son of Caesar. Especially for the Greek populations that Paul was speaking to, the restoration of Greek rule would have been an important cause. For the Greeks that believed great hero's came from the Gods, like Hercules or Agamemnon, born from Gods, this story would be the greatest Greek heroic myth of all. This is the son of Isis, the human incarnation of Horus, his mother Cleopatra, who was the Greek incarnation of Isis.

If we view Christianity as a revolutionary movement, its effectiveness becomes clear. Rome tolerated various religions but persecuted Christians, notably under Nero, who blamed them for the Great Fire of Rome. Nero, the last Julian Caesar, saw Christianity facilitate the Flavians' rise to power, replacing the Julian dynasty as the new Caesars. In 325 AD, the Neo-Flavian Caesar Constantine established the Catholic Church and founded Constantinople, effectively shifting Rome's center to the East. By 410 AD, the Visigoths, Arian Christians, sacked Rome. This history highlights Christianity's utility as a revolutionary force, or as Constantine described it, a religion for conquerors.

7. In the New Testament, Jesus asks his disciples, "But who do you say that I am?" This question appears in the Gospel of Matthew 16:15, Mark 8:29, and Luke 9:20 in slightly different forms.

Jesus asks this question to prompt his disciples to declare their understanding of his identity. Often referred to as the "Confession of Peter," as Peter responds by saying, "You are the Messiah, the Son of the living God" (Matthew 16:16).

Especially at this time in Palestine, the living God is Caesar. If the message was coming from Caesarion, it would be crucial for nobody to know who he was, they would be sure to never actually say who. If he were the son of Caesar, that would get you killed. Most would never know who he really was, and if Rome knew they would re-kill him.

"Then he ordered his disciples not to tell anyone that he was the Messiah." Matthew 16:20

Other than to say he was the Son of God, Christ never actually says who he is.

In addition this is a strange and cryptic question, Christ had been baptized by John the Baptist, at that point he was declared the Son of God, then in John 4:25–26, he tells a woman he is the Messiah. So why keep asking this question when the fact that he is the Son of God and the Messiah is common knowledge.

8. He knows more than the Pharisees. If he was Caesarion, he would have been very well taught in all the mysteries and religions, especially his own.

9. Caesarion's parents were killed over money and power. Wealth is not the way to salvation, rather, it is absurd and opposes salvation, every good Platonist, Stoic, and Cynic knows this.

It does beg the question, why has Caesarion been omitted from our common history, since it is so fitting to the history of Christ. In Church we are never told of the geopolitical elements of the period, this is similar to telling a story about Winston Churchill without mentioning Hitler, or a World War.

Consider the political thinking within the early first century Roman empire. Julius Caesar had been killed, Cleopatra, and the Greek Macedonian Ptolemaic Pharaohs were also dead, Caesar Augustus had made Egypt his personal property, and taken control of Israel. He had installed Herod Antipas as Tetrarch of Galilee and Perea, and Israel would become a client state of the Romans. As before, Herod rules through the help of Pharisees, the priest class would control the population for the ruling power as was done for the Greek Macedonian rulers, and before that of the Persians, and before that for the Egyptians.

What is obvious, if you read the Old Testament, is that Abraham and his men are mercenaries, and that Israel is a military institution that will defend whosoever is in power. We will see Israel fight for Greek interests until it turns sides in favor of Rome, supporting the new line of Caesars, the Flavians. Today Israel remains in support of Rome, rather a Roman Catholic Western Corporate Alliance.

These three truths can explain much about the military purpose of Israel, and may explain why the Jews are so central to the Roman Catholic message ...

1. If God gives land to the Jews, then Egypt, or the Empire of the day must permit and defend the transfer.

2. Unless Israel is supported by a larger outside economy, Egypt will always dominate over Israel.

3. Israel is an ideally located military defensive position to protect the wealth generated by the Nile River valley, and today to control the wealth generated by Middle East oil.

Since most people don't read, and history is a story told by those in power, it is not difficult to obscure important facts.

In the conflict between Greek and Roman rule, the child Caesarean, with his dual Roman-Greek parentage would be the most logical historical person to fill the shoes of Christ. After all, in the eyes of many people within the empire, he is the "son of God," regardless if Christ was, or was not the son of God, Caesarean was the son of two gods, Caesar and Cleopatra, at least people of that time would surely think so. If people were looking for a ruler, a divine ruler, that would bring back the Greek political status quo to the entire region, this boy would have been their first choice. Nonetheless, Caesarean is not mentioned in history, at least not the history we are told today.

Today the message we hear in Church omits this monumental Greek-Roman conflict. But to the known world at the time of Christ this conflict would have been most important to everyone. Also take into account that in the ancient world everything is viewed and understood through a religious or theological point of view.

Although little is known of Jesus Christ in the first century, the Apostle Paul, and a rising Christian movement will definitely make Christ a key figure for this period of history.

In light of how useful religion is to tie an empire together, here are three possibilities for the story of Jesus.

1. It is exactly true as written in the Bible. Three wise men, Magi, (Persian Zoroastrian Priests) who foretell through astronomical events or astrological omens, the birth of Christ king of the Jews. Christ was the virgin birth son of God, and was God. He was the son of a carpenter and was self taught. He became the teacher for a non-violent religious movement that ended with its leader's crucifixion, and the destruction of the Jewish Temple. An account that must be accepted by faith.

2. It never happened and was invented by Paul and other co-conspirators. Invented to effect change in these troubled times. Paul was a Roman citizen, a Jew, and from Tarsus. He would have had cause to do this. As a Roman citizen the new political changes would mean that the populations that were once the Hellenistic and Aramaic world of Egypt, Persia, and Greece would now be under the Latin control of Rome. Paul a Roman, if allied to the new Flavian Caesars, would have had good reason to formulate a Jewish centered religion for the new empire, a religion that would incorporate the Greek Platonic concept of an unknowable God, the Soul, and the Trinity.

These words describe the Platonic concept of the "ONE," the unknowable God, and certainly do not agree with Genesis:

The Son is the image of the invisible God, the firstborn over all creation. For in him all things were created: things in heaven and on earth, visible and invisible, whether thrones or powers or rulers or authorities; all things have been created through him and for him. He is before all things, and in him all things hold together. Colossians 1:15-17

Paul, was the apostle to the gentiles and crucial in spreading Christianity, and forming its core theological concepts. The Jews of his time had been in a long war against the Romans. Paul's home of Tarsus, where Anthony and Cleopatra had come together to fight for the control of Rome, was the capital of Cilicia, which had been conquered by Rome in 67 BC.

Nero was the last Caesar of the Julian family, and tradition holds that St. Paul's death was perhaps part of the executions of Christians ordered by him following the great fire in the city, in 64 CE. If it is true that the Apostle Paul was connected to the violent revolution in Rome, then it is possible he was using the new faith of Christ as rebellious propaganda.

The Flavian dynasty that comes after Nero, also has cause to produce both unrest, and anti-Nero propaganda.

The Flavian Dynasty is directly tied to the First Jewish-Roman War. Vespasian was sent to suppress the Jewish revolt (66–73 CE), but he used this campaign as a power base to launch his own bid for Caesar during Rome's civil war in 69 CE. After Vespasian became emperor, his son Titus finished crushing the Jewish revolt, securing both Roman authority and the legitimacy of their new dynasty.

Christianity became the instrument of peace and control, a creed to pacify the Jewish unrest and unite a theologically diverse empire under one faith.

A unique aspect of the Jesus Logos, is that it is very similar to that of Zoroastrianism, the religion of St. Paul's birthplace, Tarsus. This is the same religion of the Persian, Cirus the Great, who was the first messiah of the Jews. As in Christianity, Zoroastrianism consists of one God Ahura Mazda, an evil Satan figure named Angra Mainyu, a Pleroma of angels, an end time battle between good and evil, and with Mithra, a Christ like figure, as the mediator. The cult of Mithra, a Zoroastrian sect, is the dominant mystery religion of first century Roman soldiers and bureaucrats.

3. It is the return of the child of Caesar and Cleopatra. The actual son of God, in fact the son of two Gods. Cleopatra and Julius Caesar, the son of God, and God, if you will. Cleopatra was the personification of Isis and her son was that of Horus, so he would have been Horus to the Egyptians, Sophia to the Greek Platonists, Caesar to the Romans, and Christ the Messiah to the Jews.

He returns to teach others to love their enemies, and rebuilds his kingdom based on love of neighbor. A God incarnate, who has renounced his wealth, and comes to love the oppressed. Comes to teach and rebuild the soul of man... to set mankind free... to tell all the truth. He professes that people must know the truth, for if they do, the world will change and will bring forth a new era. This could be the explanation for the Q source, and the "Teacher of Righteousness" spoken of in the Dead Sea Scrolls.

Power is maintained through the alliances of families and their children, and it would stand to reason that the royal family of Cleopatra would have intermarried with the Jewish Kings to maintain alliances. This child would also be a descendant of King David. That would make his mother Jewish and he would be Jewish as well.

When Herod Antipas became king of Judea in 4 BC, Caesarian would have been 51, just entering his years of wisdom. If, as his mother had ordered, he was sent to India, he would have spent his teenage years on the far edge of the old Persian Empire, where the belief in one God, central to Zoroastrianism, was deeply rooted.

Zoroastrianism, the Persian faith, was a monotheistic religion devoted to one creator God, built upon a dualistic struggle between good and evil, and prophesying a final triumph of good at the end of time. This faith later influenced the Book of Revelation, which was included in the New Testament canon by the Council of Hippo in 393 AD and the Council of Carthage in 397 AD. A contradiction within itself as it is a textual change of the Bible which is condemned in Revelation 22:18-19, warning against adding to or taking away words of the book.

MITHRA AND PLATONISM

The Biblical Magi or "Three Wise Men" were Zoroastrian priests. The wise men, along with all the references to Satan point to a Zoroastrian influence within the New Testament. Christianity is an independent Jewish Minyan, based on an Old Testament which was not dualistic, and has little concern for an evil demigod. Yet the New Testament is filled with references to Satan which sound very similar to the Zoroastrian enemy of Ahura Mazda, Angra Mainyu (meaning 'destructive spirit'). For the Zoroastrians, Angra Mainyu is the originator of death and all that is evil in the world.

It would be incomprehensible that the Apostles who wrote in Greek, or in particular Paul who was from the Greek/Persian city of Tarsus where Mithraism was practiced, would have been unaware of these striking similarities to the Zoroastrian faith, and its secretive sect the Cult of Mithra.

The city of Tarsus was located in the Roman province of Cilicia. Plutarch, a Greek historian who lived from 46 to 120 AD, wrote that the Cilician pirates in 68 BC worshiped Mithras, however, it is not clear whether this refers to the Persian god Mithras or to a local deity. There is no archaeological evidence to support the claim that Mithraism originated in Tarsus, but we know it was prevalent there. Some scholars believe that Mithraism originated in Persia and spread to the Roman Empire through trade routes. Others believe that it originated in the Roman Empire and spread to Persia.

In any case the Apostle Paul of all people must have known the similarity of the Christian apocalyptic logos to that of the Zoroastrian end times, seen Satan as Angra Mainyu, and God as Ahura Mazda.

Mithraism stands out as the most secret and least known religion, and as secrecy is the best tool for those who wish to hold power, if we hope to understand the origins of Christianity, we should look to the cult of Mithra, carefully.

PRECESSION OF THE EQUINOXES

Prior to the first century we understood the stars as fixed in the sky within 12 constellations that move with the seasons. We only knew of 7 objects that moved separately to the heavens, 5 planets, plus the moon and the sun. These were Gods to most people on earth, Saturn, Jupiter, Mars, Venus, and Mercury. The fixed stars on the other hand were souls, what motivated the material world, inhabited each of us and gave us life. When we died our Soul would return to the heavens.

In Nicaea, the same village that will give us the Council of Nicaea, and the Catholic Church, in about 150 BC, Hipparchus, a Greek astronomer and mathematician discovers something very unusual about the stars above; they are not fixed, they move in what we call the precession of the equinox. In a world who's greatest science is the study of the heavens, this new information would have been transformative.

I believe that the Cult of Mithra was a secret religion that developed from the observations of Hipparchus, and combined elements of the Roman cult of Sol Invictus, and Zoroastrianism.

This new observation makes not only a new religion, but a new calendar which will have some 26,000 years, that will repeat on the anniversary of what?

In first-century Rome, the true turning point was the deification of Augustus, Son of God. The birth of Christ, though later seen as central, was hardly noticed at the time.

This new calendar is divided into 12 zodiac ages, each lasting 2,166 years, marking the 26,000-year cycle of the precession of the stars. As we approach 2024, it's clear why some rabbis and priests now claim that Revelation is near, with the current 2,166-year epoch coming to an end.

Mithra is the mediator between good and evil, the conflict between the Zoroastrian God Ahura Mazda and Angra Manyu. Mithra is the deity that controls the precession of the equinoxes along with the astrological destiny of humanity. It is likely that it was the influence of the Cult of Mithra that gave us the three wise men or Zoroastrian Magi, who astrologically foretold the birth of Christ. It is also likely that the apocalypse foretold in the New Testament also came from this cult.

For the Greek Platonists, the Roman cult of Sol Invictus, and Persian Zoroastrians, the secret cult of Mithra along with this new interpretation of the heavens would be very attractive. The Roman Cult of Mithra, working in secret could easily be the underpinning of Christianity.

CHRIST AND MITHRA

There are several instances where Mithraic temples have been repurposed or converted into Christian churches. One of the most famous examples is the Basilica of San Clemente in Rome, Italy. The current church sits atop an earlier 4th-century basilica, which was built over a Mithraic temple dating back to the 2nd century. Archaeological excavations beneath the basilica have revealed the remains of the Mithraic temple, providing evidence of the site's earlier use.

Other examples of churches built upon or near former Mithraic sites include the Church of Santa Prisca in Rome and the Church of Santa Maria Capua Vetere in Italy. In these cases, the presence of Mithraic artifacts or inscriptions in the vicinity of the churches suggests a connection to the earlier Mithraic cult.

Overall, while it is difficult to provide a precise number, it is clear that there were instances where Mithraic temples were repurposed or incorporated into Christian churches during the spread of Christianity in the Roman Empire.

If you wish to go down a rabbit hole, then consider that the cult of Mithra is still around, and that it is the bases of all modern Secret Societies, including the Catholic Church. It pretends to see in the precession of the heavens astrological markers for determining the timing of the apocalypse, and finds signals in astrology prior to acts of great importance.

Nancy Reagan was not alone in seeking astrological advice, astrology is still an important and wide spread mystical belief. By 325 AD, Christianity was divided into many separate beliefs, each influenced by different aspects of Jewish, Gnostic, and Platonic concepts. All with one core belief in Christ, a savior, with a Logos which was expected to transform humanity, yet never did.

To me, power is best held in secret, and through a religious eschatology. In The Prince, Machiavelli refers to religion as a tool of the ruler, to be used as a method by which he can convince the masses of his goodness.

> *"They are sustained by the ancient institutions of religion, which are so powerful and of such a quality that they keep their princes in power no matter how they act and live their lives."* — Niccolò Machiavelli, The Prince.

Of all the first century religions, Mithraism is the most Roman, and the exact cult I would expect the Roman Emperor Constantine to have been initiated into. It is too similar to Catholicism, too centered on power, for me not to expect that it is this religion, and the society behind it that gave us the Catholic Church through the Council of Nicea in 325 AD.

It is likely that the Apostle Paul was a good Roman, a loyal initiate of the Cult of Mithra, and the communities he would write to were of that same Cult. He promoted Christianity in order to support the new Flavian Caesars, Vespasian (69–79 AD) and his son Titus (79–81 AD), as well as to make both Jews and gentiles more servile Romans within the newly conquered territories.

The Jews have no word for religion. The Hebrew word for religion is yahadut, which means "Judaism," and first appeared in the Middle Ages. The word 'religion' itself comes from a Latin word religare, "to re-tie, or re-bind" or to "unite." The primary job of a religion is to unify people under a ruler, as was the Kingdom of David and Solomon unified under Judaism. Later the Persians under Ezra would reintroduce Judaism to the land of Israel to unify the faith for the Persian rulers. It would be reasonable to consider the Christ story was created, or later managed and promoted for political reasons, to serve Roman Caesars, as was clearly the case for the Neo-Flavian Emperor Constantine, who gave us the Council of Nicea in the 4th century, as well as the term "In hoc signo vinces."

From a political perspective, religion is a tested method for ruling a state, and one should notice that the Christian gospel has striking similarities to many of the pre-existing belief systems of the time. There are common motifs with those of Krishna, the Avatars of Vishnu, the Greek Platonic Trinity, the Persian deity Mithra, and the Egyptian God Horus, the list goes on. In order for Christianity to have the religious effect of binding people under a common belief, then, a common symbolic thread to the preexisting beliefs of the region you hope to rule would be essential.

The first century Romans under Augustus have conquered the Egyptians, Persians, and Greeks. Christianity melds the belief of all religious beliefs, it has Egyptian, Zoroastrian, Gnostic, Jewish and Platonic elements.

The more I study first-century Christianity alongside the Flavian takeover of Rome, the harder it is not to view the Apostle Paul as a Roman propagandist. Central to my belief is the fact that power is best exercised in secret, that deception is a most powerful tool in the conflict for power, and that the best way to deal with revolution is to join the revolution. I have a strong suspicion that the Apostle Paul was working within the secret Mithraic cult, to develop a religion that rallied a revolutionary following, ultimately unseating the Julian family and installing the Flavians as the new Caesars, all while unifying the empire's diverse religions under one faith centered on a Jewish Messiah and its Old Testament God.

JOHN THE BAPTIST TO THE APOSTLE PAUL

According to the Gospel of Luke, around 28 AD, John the Baptist began his ministry of preaching and baptizing by the Jordan River, which marked the western edge of Herod Antipas' territory of Perea. John condemned Herod's marriage to Herodias as incestuous and contrary to Jewish law, since Herodias was both Herod's niece and his brother's former wife. John's growing influence among the people made Herod fearful of potential rebellion. Consequently, John was imprisoned and later executed. However, before his imprisonment, John baptized Jesus Christ, marking the beginning of the ministry of Jesus Christ.

Jesus continued to preach a message of repentance and the coming Kingdom of God, which further threatened Herod's rule. His growing following and the radical nature of his teachings added to Herod's fear of unrest and rebellion.

Consider this phrase:

"then you will know the truth, and the truth will set you free." John 8:32

But what is this truth, and what freedom does it offer? Could it have referred to freedom from Roman rule? Such a notion would certainly have been problematic for Pontius Pilate, the Roman governor of Judea.

We are often told that the ministry of Jesus Christ had undertones of resistance against Rome. However, the New Testament barely touches upon the many violent Jewish rebellions of the first century or the political struggles between the Jews, Egyptians, and the Roman Empire.

John the Baptist emerges as the fiery leader of a spiritual uprising, only to be executed by Herod Antipas for his trouble. But the revolution doesn't die with him; Jesus Christ picks up the mantle and carries the movement forward. Three decades later, as Nero's reign crumbles the Julian dynasty, an unlikely recruit joins the cause: the former persecutor-turned-evangelist, Paul the Apostle.

We have the head of John the Baptist and a public crucifixion of the body of Christ, but where is the evidence of the death of the other son of god, Caesarian?

There is significant uncertainty regarding the true intent behind the Apostle Paul's vision of Christianity. Was it a revolutionary doctrine meant to liberate the world from Roman oppression, or was it, in fact a construct of the Roman Empire within itself? Consider how Paul's teachings cleverly merge Zoroastrian apocalyptic beliefs, Greek platonic-philosophical ideas, within a Jewish scriptural context, creating an ideal new faith for the Empire, designed to pacify not only the Jewish people, but also the Greek territories Rome now held. A religion urging them to "turn the other cheek" and "love their enemies."

Furthermore, this vision did lay the groundwork for a Catholic Church that later became the State religion of Rome, and has bolstered Roman authority to this day. Consider this new faith as a sophisticated tool for controlling the subjugated Greek populations, ultimately benefiting the new Caesars, particularly the Flavians.

With so much history omitted from the New Testament, we are left to wonder: what is the real truth behind Christianity, and what was its intended message?"

The Apostle Paul's vision of the Christian religion may be a revolution to liberate the world from Roman tyranny by the incorporation of a Zoroastrian Apocalypse, and Greek Platonic concepts, into a Jewish democratic call for revolt. Or, it may be the foundation of a tyrannical Catholic Church. A clever, occult, and strategic method of control for a newly conquered Greek population, in support of the new Caesars, the Flavians.

A NEW RELIGION FOR THE EMPIRE

I've explored the idea of Caesarian as a potential historical figure for Christ, which, while intriguing, remains ultimately irrelevant to the core of Christianity. What truly matters is the message itself. The Logos presented in Christian texts mirrors essential themes from Egyptian, Greek, and Persian religious traditions, all within a Jewish framework. Christianity arose as the perfect faith to unify the diverse peoples of the Roman Empire, especially those recently subjugated under what was once Greek rule. This Logos, expressed in Greek, reflects motifs familiar to a newly conquered Greek population, binding them to the emerging Roman order.

There is no historical doubt that violent revolts against Roman rule occurred in Israel during the first century. The First Jewish Revolt (66–70 CE) began with a major uprising in Judea, culminating in the destruction of the Second Temple and the widespread dispersal of the Jewish people. However, Jewish resistance to Roman authority extended far beyond Judea.

Kitos War (115–117 CE), saw revolts erupt in Jewish communities throughout the Roman Empire, including in Cyrene, Alexandria, Cyprus, and Mesopotamia. In Cyrene, Jewish rebels, led by Lukuas, ravaged the city, and similar insurrections took place in Alexandria. Cyprus also saw significant bloodshed, prompting the Roman government to ban Jews from the island. The unrest even reached Mesopotamia, where Jewish communities rebelled against Roman forces during Emperor Trajan's campaign in the region.

These uprisings were followed by the Bar Kokhba revolt (132–136 CE), which sought to overthrow Roman authority once more, but ended in a brutal crackdown, leaving Judea devastated. This widespread pattern of resistance illustrates that Jewish opposition to Rome was not an isolated phenomenon, but part of a larger and enduring conflict, deeply intertwined with the political and religious upheavals of the time.

Amid these upheavals, the Roman general Vespasian, who put down the Jewish rebellion in Judaea for Nero, replaced the Julian family of Caesar Augustus as the ruling dynasty of Rome (69 AD). One can imagine how useful Jewish and Christian revolutionaries might have been to the Flavians as they seized control of the empire. Just as Josephus switched sides to become an ally of the Flavians, it's likely that other Jews also saw an opportunity to align themselves with the new regime, I see the Apostle Paul as one of those.

The Flavians, with Titus at the helm, would preside over an empire that was predominantly Greek in culture and population. Titus would have disseminated the Christian doctrine almost as propaganda, written in Greek, embracing multiple faiths and promoting non-violence to serve as a tool for pacifying unrest in the empire.

Joseph Atwill, in his book *Caesar's Messiah*, presents a provocative theory: that Christianity was a deliberate creation by Titus to quell the ongoing Jewish revolts. While this idea is interesting, it requires the belief that Titus, or those around him, had immense foresight. The revolutionary nature of the Christian "Logos" would not typically be something a ruler would desire his subjects to adopt, unless its design had a specific purpose, such as undermining the influence of the Julian dynasty, particularly the reign of Nero, to solidify the rise of the Flavians.

The struggle between the Julian and Flavian dynasties for control of Rome lends credence to the theory that a revolutionary religious text like Christianity could be a tool for destabilizing the Julians. Once in power, the Flavians could have used a priestly class to guard the true meaning of the text, offering only a controlled and diluted interpretation to the masses. Titus and his advisors, assuming this theory holds, would have had to trust that the general populace would never fully understand the radical demands of the Christian Logos, while the priesthood maintained its congregants within a belief that served the Roman Rulers interest.

I don't believe that the Apostles or Christ were simply created by Titus and his conspirators. I think that it is more plausible that there was a Christ, rather I think there were many Christs, the Platonic, Zoroastrian and Jewish religions were already intermixed within this new empire, there were many with messianic concepts, new concepts were exchanging from one religion to the other. From before the time of the Maccabees, Greek philosophy and religion had been infiltrating Jewish thinking.

Philo of Alexandria, also known as Philo the Jew, an Egyptian who wrote in Greek, lived between 15 BC and 41 CE, is considered to have influenced Christianity, and is also one of the best sources for Platonism. Philo would have been a contemporary of Christ, yet the fact that he never mentions Christ only demonstrates Christian thinking was prevalent in the absence of Christ, and that Christ was mostly unknown in the first century.

Titus and company converted these messages into one that would be more suitable to Roman interests, and the Council of Nicaea later consolidated the dogma, for example:

"Let everyone be subject to the governing authorities, for there is no authority except that which God has established. The authorities that exist have been established by God. Consequently, whoever rebels against the authority is rebelling against what God has instituted, and those who do so will bring judgment on themselves..." Romans 13

It could be that it was all carefully considered by Rome, and then evangelized by the Apostles, but I don't think so, rather I think there was a Christ that started a word, a logos that began to spread, then taken up by the Apostles and later tweaked to better apply to the Roman Empires interests.

Besides the obvious insertions to benefit Roman rule, the Logos of Jesus Christ appears to describe a way of life by which Rome can not subjugate Christians. A path that will work if you follow it, but one that most people will not apply to their lives.

If you give away your wealth, there is no wealth to tax.

If you "turn the other cheek" and "love your enemy," you don't fight, and if killed you have eternal life.

If you beg you take resources from Rome, enough beggars and you have destroyed the economy of the state.

If you keep these practices within a community of like minded people you will have an ideal economy of free people.

With an empire of Christians how can Rome tax or make war? But, if you include the Old Testament you will have essentially contradicted the Christian message.

The obvious may have been known, that very few people want to be poor, are unafraid of death, or can love their enemies. This would make the Christian Logos beautiful words, but impractical, but very practical if you include the Jewish war story of the Old Testament.

To become free, the Jews are told not to confide in the Pharisees who have been governing them on behalf of their Roman client. Do the Jews now know they have always been trapped within an illusion of freedom, with their kings, and their priests always as subjects of the ruling power of the day. That ever since Moses took them from Egypt their priests have projected an illusion and been the tool used to dominate them.

The Pharisees and Rome would lose grip if the Jews were told this truth. This failure of the Pharisees and the Temple, is the basis of Stevens' defense to the High Priest.

Yet the Most High does not dwell in houses made by hands, as the prophet says, Heaven is my throne, and the earth is my footstool. What kind of house will you build for me, says the Lord, or what is the place of my rest?

Did not my hand make all these things?'

You stiff-necked people, uncircumcised in heart and ears, you always resist the Holy Spirit. As your fathers did, so do you. (Acts 7: 48-51)

The passage that ends with "you always resist the Holy Spirit," suggests that the Holy Spirit is a divine force acting upon the soul, resembling the Platonic concept of the Trinity. However, this idea isn't Jewish, as Judaism has no Trinity. Scholarly consensus also holds that the Old Testament makes no mention of an immortal soul independent of the body. The fact that the Pharisees "always" resist the Holy Spirit suggests that the Platonic notions of the soul and the Trinity had been resisted for some time, this is understandable given that Israel had been under Greek dominion since Alexander, for over 300 years.

In Christian theology, the Holy Spirit is the third part of the Trinity, while the soul is distinct yet interconnected. The soul is often seen as the essence of an individual, their mind, will, emotions, and spiritual core. The Holy Spirit, by contrast, is viewed as God's presence within and around believers, guiding, empowering, and transforming their lives.

Another clearly Cynical, Stoic and Platonic aspect of the Christian logos is that it makes clear that wealth, and our attachment to material things is a serious problem...

Again I tell you, it is easier for a camel to go through the eye of a needle than for a rich man to enter the kingdom of God." Matthew 19:24

It is easier for a camel to go through the eye of a needle than for a rich man to enter the kingdom of God." Mark 10:25

Indeed, it is easier for a camel to go through the eye of a needle than for a rich man to enter the kingdom of God." Luke 18:25

People who love their enemies, and accept poverty are ideal for any tyrant, but if they govern themselves that may be a problem, since the tyranny falls apart if they go to Ekklesia to govern themselves, like the Amish!

Of course the Christian message must be ignored by those in power, rulers will still rule over their servants and slaves.

Christianity remains an excellent message for tyranny, it gives slaves a sense of power in the afterlife, acceptance of their poverty, and eternal life as long as they are good servants. This is done while the Old Testament provides instructions for the warrior ruling class.

The Christian message is also one of equality, and since equality is the enemy of Tyrants, I don't think that when Constantine gives us the Nicene Creed in 325 AD, he personally adopts this belief, clearly he sees this Creed as the ideal religion for dominion within a master-slave social paradigm. He correctly chose Christianity as Romes new State religion, and has ruled the West to this day.

Even today, those who seek to rule or wield influence over others understand these principles as undeniable truths:

> *One should not embellish or dress up Christianity: it has waged a war to the death against this higher*

type of man, it has excommunicated all the fundamental instincts of this type, it has distilled evil, the Evil One, out of these instincts — the strong human being as the type of reprehensibility, as the 'outcast'. Christianity has taken the side of everything weak, base, ill-constituted, it has made an ideal out of opposition to the preservative instincts of strong life; it has depraved the reason even of the intellectually strongest natures by teaching men to feel supreme values of intellectually as sinful, as misleading, as temptations. Nietzsche: The Anti-Christ

"Thus it is well to seem merciful, faithful, humane, sincere, religious, and also to be so; but you must have the mind so disposed that when it is needful to be otherwise you may be able to change to the opposite qualities. And it must be understood that a prince, and especially a new prince, cannot observe all those things which are considered good in men, being often obliged, in order to maintain the state, to act against faith, against charity, against humanity, and against religion. And, therefore, he must have a mind disposed to adapt itself according to the wind, and as the variations of fortune dictate, and, as I said before, not deviate from what is good, if possible, but be able to do evil if constrained." — Niccolò Machiavelli, The Prince

GOOD AND EVIL THE FLAW OF CHRISTIANITY

Shakespeare famously wrote in Hamlet, "For there is nothing either good or bad, but thinking makes it so." He correctly states that good and evil are mental constructs that apply only if we think about a condition from our point of view.

Good and evil describe contrasting aspects of existence which apply to moral and ethical decisions, behaviors, and intentions of individuals, societies, and institutions. The words are used to judge actions and events, from personal conduct to historical occurrences and cultural narratives.

In mythology, and religion, good and evil symbolize the struggle between virtue and vice, order and chaos, or harmony and discord. These concepts have been integral in shaping moral frameworks and guiding principles across our culture.

It is crucial to recognize that these concepts are cultural judgments, not decrees of any divine reality. Yet in Western faith, they have been elevated into a false framework in which human behavior is attributed to spiritual forces, such as a good God and an evil Satan, rather than to our own choices and cultural constructs.

Good and evil as divine concepts may seem obvious, but this is only because we are conditioned to see the world this way. This misconception is dangerous, and it underpins many flaws in our society. Western faith casts God as the ultimate arbiter of good and Christ as the redeemer who carries our sins, while Satan becomes the eternal adversary. In doing so, religion obscures human responsibility, offering a convenient scapegoat for evil and a divine justification for obedience. Worse still, it constructs a grand apocalyptic narrative in which these forces clash at the end of time, embedding the logic of perpetual conflict and religiously sanctioned war.

The nature of evolution is our sexuality, which makes us inherently competitive beings. Good and evil are the words we use to define and contrast the outcome of this competition, it is only a point of view of an outcome of a competitive struggle, what is considered good to one party may be considered evil by the other.

This is misunderstood in most all religious text, as there is an attempt to see good and evil as divine forces that can be controlled only if you follow the instructions of your Priest. The contrast between good and evil, is a scare tactic used by religious institutions to manipulate and condition social behavior.

For the oppressed, it is clear good is preferred over evil, and when found helpless against oppression it is natural to see ones oppression as a spiritual force, it is understandable that one may seek comfort by calling for the assistance of a good God, as you can see no other solution. This false perception causes inaction against the perpetrator, as one prays that God will intervene. Evil is corrected not by God, evil can only be corrected by education and a logical and proper response to the situation.

Consider the civil rights movement in the United states, the proper action or "good" was protest and defiance, along with the reeducation of the general population of the need for equal rights. But, do we consider why rights were abridged and was that "evil"?

Within the context of slavery, methods such as whipping, starvation, and all other forms of punishment are viewed as evil by slaves. However, the slave master might perceive these actions as good and necessary for managing labor. Evil is not a Divine issue but rather a problem of intellect, education, perception, or simply a mistaken point of view.

For those in power evil is a necessity, for it must be an acceptable norm if you wish to stay in power. Ultimately, if you rule over others, you are involved in the act of subjugation, and subjugation is the basis of slavery which is the foundational evil Moses frees his people from.

The first century Platonists saw no divine or spiritual conflict between good an evil, nor do the Jews have an evil Satan, whereas the Zoroastrians definitely do. This is why I believe that the Zoroastrian astrological Cult of Mithra, with Mithra as the mediator between good and evil, its priest who were called Father, and communion meal, was the secret religion of the Apostle Paul, the Emperor Constantine, and to this day is the true secret Cult behind the power of the Catholic Church. The Good vs Evil perception has been central to our western religion, and is the primary mistake of western thinking.

Our interpretation of Good and Evil was derived from our "collective will," which comes from the competitive nature of civilization. Good is often personified as the weak and meek, while Evil is seen as a force that attacks what is good, the meek and weak, embodying the victor or superior as Evil. Within the framework of Western religious belief, this dynamic forces rulers into the role of Satanists, while the servant class becomes the meek who must be oppressed. This conception underpins our Western understanding of competition and power.

These ideas are instilled in us from a young age through religious teachings, and as adults they are reinforced through secret societies within the more dominant sectors of society.

The Christian Good versus Evil divine conflict fails to appreciate the very nature of the Platonic Nous or Intelligence, the emanation of the Unknowable God which the Soul through the Holy Spirit strives to know.

For the Platonist, evil is only the lack of intelligence or nous. This is seen as a failure of the Soul in its attempt to know God, (God which is what is Good}, through the Nous. Plato used the word *"nous"* as understood to the common everyday Greek, which simply meant "good sense" or "awareness," which is the same as intelligence to us. Therefore if you have developed your intelligence and have good sense you simply do not do evil. Good is natural and normal behavior and evil is simply what fools do, having no relationship to any divine forces.

The Christian Logos had hoped to produce the ideal community, maybe even to have transformed the world, but in my opinion it has this flaw, the conflict between good and evil.

While Christianity may have been effective within monastic communities, it has not transformed society at large.

Historically, the Catholic Church has not been interested in the poor, it has always been a tyranny led by the aristocracy, Christianity has been from its inception a tool for conquest. The Church assumed a role akin to that of the Pharisees, transforming the Logos into an instrument of ecclesiastical power. It defended the authority of monarchs and the power they wielded over the subjugated and the meek.

Humanity is a species driven to evolve by sexual dominance, often too proud to acknowledge its true animal nature. We exist within a deterministic framework, devoid of free will, which makes the concept of good and evil even more absurd.

The concepts of good and evil are constructs designed to instill fear in the ignorant and empower those in authority. Until we recognize how determined our behavior is, we will never change. We will always kill the Messiah, only to crown the next dominant hairless ape.

GOOD AND EVIL WITHIN JUSTICE

We all claim to know what justice is, yet humanity has never agreed on its true definition. In modern democracies, the promise of equal justice is an illusion, as is democracy itself. The modern democracy is clandestinely managed by tyrannical secret societies that operate on a "justice of the strong" paradigm. What we call equal justice is merely a well-organized deception.

Our judicial system is set to guarantee that if you have money, lawyers, and influence, you will prevail and that without them, you will fail. Therefore, in a society replete with secret societies judicial success demands becoming a loyal servant to the secret society that controls the court and political order. Your duty will now be to the "justice of the strong," to favor your brothers and harm all others. This is the reason democracy failed in ancient Greece and why modern democracy can feel more like an illusion than reality. Tyranny, or concentrated power in secrecy, is simply a far more efficient path to control.

"Justice is nothing other than the advantage of the stronger," Thrasymachus, Plato, The Republic

Power is defined by strength, and the most effective path to it has always been through harming others while showing loyalty only to your kin, clan, or political order. In the modern democracy, secret societies take the place of clans, and their secrecy make them far more effective. While this is a brutally effective precept for building a nation, it has also been the direct cause of our endless wars, and societies built on human enslavement. Socrates creates the argument that the "justice of the strong" is wrong, that we can live in a society of rules and laws equal to all. So we killed him.

Christ adds democracy and a divine nature to the Socratic argument of equal justice. So we certainly killed him as well.

You can see evolution in history, just as you've seen it in your own life, from childhood into adulthood. But the kind of evolution that matters now is no longer biological, it is intellectual. Knowledge, education, and reason paves the path of both our past and future. It has been a bloody, difficult and long journey from hairless apes to today, yet we still function through our primal primate behavior. The path forward will require recognition of our evolutionary animal behavior, plus greater truth and honesty, two aspects that are hard for most to muster, yet this is the only equation to achieve the wisdom required to cure what we call evil, the only path to redemption.

Our history has been soaked in blood, shaped more by false opinions than by truth. We have inched away from dogma toward reason, and though progress is real, we easily backslide. We no longer cheer gladiators in arenas, but quarterbacks on fields; the barbarism is less direct, yet still here. Democracy and justice is a mask draped over the machinery of power. Yet, however haltingly, the trajectory points toward greater freedom for mankind.

Evolution now calls us to something greater, a conscious step beyond our illusion. Not salvation offered by an external god, but redemption through truth. We must confront the absurdity of a world where conscious beings enslave and kill, not for truth or meaning, but for power. Why do we cause endless suffering? Why do we continue to bring new lives into conflict we can neither justify nor explain? Religion offers us only scapegoats, myths, and promises; any hope lies in our ability to reason and find logic in our acts.

Only with logic guided by reason, and humbled by our own blatant absurdity, can we finally take another step forward to civilize our base instincts, to govern our tribal impulse, and to build a future worthy of a species that has become the crown of evolution on earth..

GOD IN AN UNJUST WORLD

I believe that equal justice can only exist when we all understand that there are two definitions for the word. In a world where the 'justice of the strong' always prevails, our belief in 'equal justice' is ultimately an illusion, a clever ploy that masks a deeper injustice. Shattering this illusion demands a fundamental revolution in thought, a new belief system, or rather, a new religion built on a clear-eyed understanding of humanity.

Since words like Good, Evil, and God are mental constructs, God can be made to fit any world view, just or unjust. Therefore, it is up to us to define and believe in a God that leads to a just world.

Our present conception of God is not pure or original but a composite, part war god, part Platonic ideal of the divine, and part Zoroastrian dualism of good and evil.

It is easy to declare there is no God, but difficult to argue that compassion is unwise. This reveals a fundamental truth: treating one another with goodness builds a better world, regardless of religious belief. Yet understanding this is only the first step. The more difficult lesson is that compassion must not be mistaken for weakness. To protect what is good, one must sometimes be resolute, unyielding. even ruthless. True humility is not fear; it is strength that needs no boasting. And meekness is not foolishness; it is a deliberate choice of restraint, not an absence of courage.

The problem with our faith is it has many inaccuracies, and it offers mixed messages. The God of the Old Testament is a ruthless ruler, while the God of the New Testament calls for meekness and service. This divides us, builds a society that rewards the ruthless with power and leaves the meek in servitude.

We need to be realistic about ourselves. We are flawed animals with base desires and troubled minds, we are only one step above a Bonobo. If we look honestly at our nature, then the idea that we are made in "God's image," is absurd.

We must be realistic about God. If God is infinite and eternal, then the gap between us and God is far greater than the gap between a human and an ant. By definition, such a being is beyond our ability to know or understand.

The world often lacks justice, ethics, and humanity. But our ability to recognize their opposites, injustice, cruelty, and inhumanity, is precisely what gives us the power to act and to do better.

The first step is to recognize that the fault lies within us. Whether we admit it or not, we are the problem. We all carry a touch of narcissism, convincing ourselves that we are fine and without serious flaws, yet in truth we are far more imperfect than we realize.

Stop asking the God's to fix our failures, stop blaming God or the devil for our faults. The path to heaven may not be dependent on good works, but here on earth the problems are caused by you, and if you don't think, if you don't act, you are the problem.

We live in an age of surplus, God has given us all that is required for each of us to have contentment, we are limited only by ignorance, and the fact that in our daily lives we face some of us who will constantly take our efforts as their spoils. The solution for these two issues is education, and an ability to keep a keen eye on corruption. To achieve this outcome I have suggested an open democratic form of governance coupled with a religion based on truth.

Recent discoveries of Gnostic documents have revealed that, first century Judaism and early Christianity existed in many forms. There wasn't just one unified Logos but various interpretations on a similar theme. The New Testament, which has been used for nearly two thousand years, was a compiled product of Emperor Constantine in 325 AD, a state religion.

This Bible, a distillation of diverse beliefs, was crafted to maintain dominion over a slave class and preserve a master-slave hierarchy.

Over the years, many texts that conflicted with the empire's chosen doctrine were either omitted or destroyed. The Bible, which many use as their life guide, is a carefully crafted manual designed to control an uninitiated, uninformed, and uneducated slave class, who tragically believe they are free and destined for heaven. Much of what is wrong with human behavior stems from misguided beliefs, and many of these failings can be traced back to Biblical teachings. If we ever hope to improve society, we must confront the flaws in these beliefs, then from this build a practical Logos for our society.

7. Opinion: The Failures of Christianity

No matter how you wish to interpret the connection between history and Western religion, the New Testament stands as a theological and philosophical framework for governance that has failed the poor and uneducated for over 2,000 years. While Christianity may have aimed to inspire social change and liberate the oppressed, it instead became a tool for tyrants and those who thrive on dominating a subjugated class. Nations do not practice love of neighbor; instead, we venerate power, oppressing the meek and kindhearted. Those who were meant to find salvation in the Christian message have become the indoctrinated masses we exploit in an economy based on a master-slave paradigm.

The reason why Christianity has been a religion of war and conquest is because the master-slave behavior is in our human nature, as bondage is the natural outcome of sexual competition. If we think, if we reason, if we approach intelligence we will recognize the absurdity of our existence, yet what we see we are unable to change, because our tyrannical reality is in our nature. Competition is the personification of the alpha male. Competition is a primal instinct rooted in our sexual drive, which fuels evolution and shapes civilization. We must recognize this reality before any meaningful change can occur.

Our Church should have been our salvation from this absurdity, but it is a monolith of dogma. It is not open to reason, it is tyrannical and was never designed to truly fulfill a Christian message. Rather its design was to make a slave population docile and subservient, to support Caesar, the vast variety of Kings and Nobility of Europe, and today corporate oligarchs.

"And when they could not find them, they dragged Jason and some of the brothers before the city authorities, shouting, **"These men who have turned the world upside down** *have come here also, and Jason has received them, and they are all acting against the decrees of Caesar, saying that there is another king, Jesus." Acts 17:*

Nothing changed, everything remains upside down, truth buried beneath illusion, and justice perverted into a farce.

If we could see the absurdity of our lives and redefine love as infinite compassion and empathy, instead of the desires we focus on today, our perspective would shift. If we recognized human existence as a collection of unnecessary suffering, we might finally understand the need to care for the least among us, instead of offering them the neglect and abuse they face now. We must stop pretending we can comprehend the unknowable, like the nature of God, and avoid labeling it as either good or evil.

Blinded by ignorance, we blame the devil for our failures and accept the absurdity of life as Gods will. We claim to be made in the image of a good God, but fail to recognize we are animals, driven by the same evolutionary instincts as apes. We fight and kill over resources, subjugate those we claim to love, and remain clueless about our true motivations or purpose, all while killing women and children in pursuit of power and land. We ignore the Christian message of love of neighbor as unrealistic, instead we accept the Old Testament model of a chosen people who strive to be so through war and aggression.

> *"The Sermon on the Mount was so "radical that the Defense Department wouldn't survive its application." 2006 speech -Sen. Barack Obama*

It is no longer inconceivable to build the world hoped for in the Christian message. Although class struggle has been how humans have moved forward and evolved, the norm is to the ideal and we will eventually come to this ideal.

Every rational person understands that we all benefit when our neighbors are intelligent and wise, and that there is no need for a leisure class or slaves to provide for them. Our economies already produce more than enough food and shelter for everyone; what we truly lack is truth and a proper education.

Progress, in the traditional sense, is over for us. There is no further evolution for humanity, intelligence will become artificial, and evolution will continue increasing complexity until reality becomes even more incomprehensible. Our purpose, as it once was, is complete. The struggle is finished. Now, it is our responsibility to build a just and humane society.

A civilization is built on its beliefs, and we will never escape the need for religion, as it is the tool that shapes our worldview. However, our civilization has outgrown its current dogma. Our belief systems are no longer compatible with modern knowledge, history, or science.

Pastors can no longer fully believe what they preach, and if they do, it leads to a case of the blind leading the blind. If we continue to cling to the status quo, we will continue to perpetuate a polarized society, divided between the ignorance of the masses and the hypocrisy of the elite.

We cannot simply abolish Western religion for some new-age concept. Any transition must preserve the past while guiding us toward a solution that truly fulfills or redeems the promises in our religious texts.

Since civilization is rooted in its beliefs, many of our problems likely stem from misunderstanding the truth about the unknown, what we call God. The solution lies in accepting that

God is unknowable, while recognizing that what we seek from God is already within reach, attainable by all, and simple to realize.

The final verse of the New Testament contains an ironic warning not to change the Word of God. The irony stems from the fact that scholars agree this passage was a later addition, not appearing until after the Council of Nicaea, more than 300 years after Christ.

What we use as our Testament did have text added, and was altered, it is a specific construct for dominion of the poor rather than its salvation. Yet, this is unimportant because the true message of an expected Messiah and the Logos is a truth which is instinctively known to all reasonable people. In other words, rational minds selected the text to be the Christian spiritual guide, and it went through editing and revisions to become the ideal Logos for tyranny, for Caesar, and today will require rational minds to give it a full revision in order for it to become a message that actually works for all mankind.

If the new and old testament has served us for this many years why could we not evolve our interpretation of the text into a more truthful version of the human reality. Certainly if we do we can then commence with the initiation of the Messianic Age that has been so awaited for.

Each of us as humans have similar motivations, and it has been from these motivations that we built the structure of our religion, society and its laws. What can we honestly ask of God that we can not provide for ourselves?

In that they show the work of the Law written in their hearts, their conscience bearing witness, and their thoughts alternately accusing or else defending them, Romans 2:14

In the past, a pantheon of gods, symbolized by planets and stars, was used to explain the mystical forces of nature. These gods were thought to influence human traits, with love and war being expressions of their will in relation to humanity, all interpreted and mediated by a priestly class.

With Christ, however, we are introduced to Platonic ideas: an unknowable God, the Logos (Son or Intellect), and the Holy Spirit, which links us to the divine. This shift calls for the removal of the priestly intermediaries, ignores celestial bodies, and places the responsibility on each individual to understand God through their own soul, applying a law focused on the well-being of others.

Recognizing that the New and Old Testaments reflect two distinct theologies could serve as a foundation for rethinking our beliefs and practices.

Competition is effective albeit brutal, throughout the world people compete, we exalt competition, a behavior which is based on taking something called profit from another.

The reason we see so few people living under a law that is directed to the benefit of neighbors is because we have chosen to do the opposite, we choose to compete, therefore we live in an absurd society based on good and evil, greed and competition, we live in misery, and we produce misery only because we choose to do nothing about these facts.

The reason we choose to compete is because it is our narcissistic nature, and although reasonable people may choose otherwise, it is not natural to be reasonable, for reason requires education, and unfortunately not everyone has this opportunity.

I don't expect people to stop competing, but I do believe that there are reasonable educated people that can see that life is better served in service to others, people that see a better world and are not motivated by the shiny objects that we obtain through competition. There are people that find it unpleasant to be motivated by sexual desire and find greater pleasure in the aesthetic values of a better society.

I call on these people, the rational, and considerate, to come together and build a proper belief and factual reality for the future.

Constantine discovered the value of Christianity as a tool for dominion, and would build a Church that would dominate the western world. A new priest class, and universal belief that was ideal for the empire. Today's Rome is not the city of Rome, but an institution that extends from the pastor of the local Church to the international cabal of rulers that profit from human toil, all fueled by our stupidity. In all these years since Jesus Christ, humanity has evolved and prospered, yet little has changed in the relation between slave, and master. It has been our Church that has carefully maintained this status quo.

Father, forgive them; for they do not know what they are doing.' And they cast lots to divide his clothing" Luke 23:34

Human evolution has been characterized by a brutal competition among hairless apes, a process we now refer to as civilization. This barbarism has been perpetuated by a Church that acts out of ignorance rather than understanding.

Our church or religion can only promote what people are willing to accept, and people can only accept what their intellectual capacity allows. Therefore, if we truly desire a better world, it becomes essential to elevate the consciousness of everyone.

"The only good is knowledge, and the only evil is ignorance."
— Socrates

Our plight stems from our ignorance of our reality, and only through proper reasoning can we hope to transcend this absurdity. Rather than reacting impulsively to life, we must engage in thoughtful contemplation of our situation, if we do, we can avoid being controlled by governments, others, or circumstances.

8. Universal Christianity: A New Faith for a New Age

The genesis of Christianity is best understood as a synthesis of predominant Hellenistic and Near Eastern traditions. It amalgamated the Egyptian preoccupation with the afterlife, the

Zoroastrian cosmic struggle between good and evil, and Platonic philosophy concerning the soul and a transcendent deity, while being fundamentally structured by a Jewish worldview and the scriptures of the Old Testament.

Judaism and Christianity, though often seen as connected, are fundamentally different. Judaism presents a war history and a guide for a "chosen people," while Christianity offers a philosophical messianic hope for the oppressed. Yet, both have been woven together into a singular doctrine that has shaped the governance of Western society.

The Old Testament gives us a dogma for a managerial-mercenary class, the "Chosen People." The added Christian message serves to attract followers, and will indoctrinate a meek and well behaved servant class, thereby acting as the managing platform for the master servant paradigm our civilization has always had.

It is essential to recognize Judaism and Christianity as independent faiths, with Judaism naturally rejecting Christian teachings. From a Christian theological standpoint, however, the inclusion of the Hebrew Bible as the "Old Testament" meant the assimilation of the "Chosen People" concept into its own dogma. The result of this assimilation was the reinforcement of a distinct, divinely-ordained group possessing a unique authority. This effectively cast the Jewish people in a permanent, "managerial" role within the Christian narrative, a group to be both respected and protected as a core tenet of the faith.

Although the New Testament says:

> *But you are a chosen people, a royal priesthood, a holy nation, a people belonging to God, that you may declare the praises of him who called you out of darkness into his wonderful light. 1 Peter 2:9–12*

Most Churches will preach the chosen status of the Jewish people.

As Pope John Paul II said,

"Jews are our elder brothers" in the faith.

Through this construct Jews can be placed in administrative positions and do the unpleasant tasks that would otherwise be done by the ruling elite, taxation, war, justice of the strong, interest and banking, etc. This method of obfuscation and governance permits the ruling elites, royal families and the like, to wipe their hands of the many dirty deeds that must take place when power acts as it must in the exploitation of a lower servant class.

The original example for this is seen in the crucifixion of Christ where the blame is taken on by the Jewish authority, as Rome washes its hands of the killing. Today we can see this in Gaza, as the United States washes its hands of a genocide, blaming a rogue Jewish state for the killing. This methodology of governance is what has given us the sad history of pogroms over the many years of western history.

Here in essence is why I see Christianity as malicious. The message of the New Testament is a wonderful attraction for a servant-slave class as it promises benevolence along with an escape from servitude, albeit in an afterlife, or after some hoped for apocalyptic future time.

By combining the Old testament with the New Testament into the Bible, we have created a recruitment tool within Christianity for the more sociopathic elements that are required to manage our master-slave social order. Christian congregants who show promise as "masters" can be selected for initiation into secret societies that will tend to be tyrannical, antinomian, and Old Testament in thinking.

Consider the potential: Secret societies target Christians who naturally disregard "turning the other cheek," instilling in them a callous, "what-do-you-care" attitude. Through this they are indoctrinated into the master class that governs us, thus forging a highly effective managerial elite. This gives us a hidden tyrannical order separate from our government, that lies within the military, police, finance, and corporate class. In essence this is what we sometimes call the "deep state," an occult behind the scenes form of governance.

The phrase "making good men better" depends greatly on your definition of "good", and draws attention to the vast importance of the meaning of this word.

For many, and for all of history power is seen as an important goal, and making men good is making them powerful, yet it has been established that power is not for the meek or kindhearted. In addition, consider that the meek are generally the same as the uneducated, kind, and law abiding fools that work hard to be good people, unaware that power is both ruthless and deceptive. Traditionally, power has been intent on slavery, the cultivation, and harvesting of labor from a docile labor class. Therefore Obama may have been correct, it may be more accurate to say "the meek will not inherit the earth".

> *"Thus Abraham our Father, peace be with him, is the father of his pious posterity who keep his ways, and the father of his disciples and of all proselytes who adopt Judaism."*
> Rambam's Letter to Ovadiah the Convert.

Judaism is not a race of Semites, but a religion of converts, which permits anyone interested in being "Chosen," to simply convert. Over the years these two contrasting dogmas, Judaism and Christianity, have produced a sort of genetic selection mechanism, collecting traits of dominant personalities all into one religion, and the more servile into another. Excellent for the Master-Slave economies of the first and subsequent centuries, but inadequate for today.

Judaism is the religion of the Chosen People, chosen to be the mediators and mercenaries between power and servitude,

Christianity on the other hand is the religion of the uneducated, meek, and kindhearted.

If you don't want to be a master over others, or a slave to your master, the following suggestion for a religion may suit you.

Thomas Jefferson, in his "Jefferson Bible," omits the Old Testament, believing that a new nation needs a religion that seeks equal justice. He saw any belief in a "Chosen People" as contradictory to the concept of justice. Long before Jefferson, Marcion, an early Christian theologian, creator of the first canon and evangelist, established a doctrine known as Marcionism. This doctrine, part of what we call Gnosticism today, asserted that the God who sent Jesus Christ was distinct from the "vengeful" God (Demiurge) who had created the world.

> *"Marcion declared that Christianity was in complete discontinuity with Judaism and entirely opposed to the scriptures of Judaism."*

Throughout history, countless cults have emerged, creating various divergent religions. It is difficult to get two people to agree on anything, and faith in its natural state has a lot of variety, this is why a single state dogma must be enforced by torture and death. First Century Rome was far more tolerant of a variety of religions than we think. Christianity itself was a chaotic mix of religious ideas, often based on themes that were both similar and wildly different to our current dogma.

In order to have a belief that matches our hoped values of equality and justice, as well as to bring each of us closer to God, I suggest even more simplification than that offered by Thomas Jefferson.

Although most people are unaware, the Church and state have always been one institution, so, in order to keep things open and honest, lets make the Church an economic and political solution, this way the Church would never again ask for money, as it would make its own money. Congregants could work in common toward social and business goals. This could be any business, providing work for the unemployed, as well as education and training for its work force.

The Ekklesia (or Church) would be reconstituted as an online, direct democracy where mandatory transparency ensures accountability and acts as a wall to the structures that enable corruption. Because our daily lives are so deeply shaped by the pursuit of a livelihood, this shift in how economic organizations are governed would, in itself, produce significant and widespread societal benefits.

Understanding the meaning of the word "good" and seeking truth would be the core of this religion, founded not on dogma but on a rational and honest depiction of reality and the divine, through open debate.

God would be understood in the Christian- Platonic sense as unknowable. All we can say about God is the obvious, we believe in God, God is the creator, is infinite, and therefore is creating now, we exist by Gods grace, and God is good. It is understood that in an infinite evolving set there is no start point, therefore creation is seen as starting at any and every point. For our practical objectives. "now" is always the first day of creation.

How we see or understand God evolves from child to adult, therefore the concept of faith, God, or the divine is personal and different for each of us.

Accept that God and the metaphysical is unknowable, yet we believe in God through faith, and that is always a speculation.

If good and evil are reflections of personal opinion, then there must exist a transcendent, unbiased reality that defines what is truly good beyond all conflict. then God must be this pure and unbiased truth, that which defines what is actually good between conflicting notions.

The core of this faith focuses on exploring what "good" means to God, how it relates to humanity, and how it should guide the way we live our lives. Through our collective and truthful contemplation of God each community can devise the most effective and best aligned code of conduct for its people.

This religion would have two principals, along with a Trinity. All other teachings, can be found in the Bible and elsewhere, all understood at the discretion of your local "Home Church" through the open collaboration of all.

THE PRINCIPAL OF DETERMINISM

> *"In nature there is nothing contingent, but all things have been determined from the necessity of the divine nature to exist and produce an effect in a certain way."* Baruch Spinoza

To see reality as deterministic helps us escape our absurd existence, and will change our faulty concept of free will. I will not explain here why a reasonable person should see reality as deterministic, and free will as a very good illusion, but if you think you have free will, you can study the neurology and physics which has proven the deterministic nature of reality. If we accept that all actions are causal and deterministic, we cannot blame others for their transgressions, and therefore, if we are reasonable, we have no choice but to forgive others when they harm us. This will put an end to sin and convert the confessional into therapy.

Instead of a sense of vengeance against those who harm us, we can study the causal factors that produced the transgression, then engineer circumstances so that unfortunate acts will not recur, over and over again. No longer will we blame some metaphysical construct for our errors, nor falsely say we are forgiven, instead we will recognize our faults, then look for and apply solutions, thus improving society. Prisons will become institutes for personal growth, and police will become social workers.

We can love those who harm us, "for they know not what they do," love becomes an infinite pity or compassion, a force for good, the motive for the repair of mankind. In essence, this is Christ's message on the cross: our shortcomings stem not from a lack of technical or mathematical knowledge, but from a lack of self-awareness, personal skills, and a true understanding of purpose. Simply put, most of us do not know how to live harmoniously with ourselves or others.

If reality is deterministic, can we change what tomorrow will bring?

I believe that changes in awareness, and fundamental shifts in how we perceive reality, is as close as we can come to free will. Our self-perception and understanding of reality shape how we respond to future events. In other words, our beliefs create the deterministic path that we refer to as our future.

Repairing the human condition can be done through the ability to forgive, converting the idea of an "eye for an eye" to one of engineered solutions. If we believe that existence is deterministic, then there can be no sin, and forgiveness is unnecessary. The solution for what we had once called sinful or evil is to simply fix the problem, and we are certainly clever enough to do that.

THE PRINCIPAL OF SEXUAL COMPETITION

A key to improving the human condition lies in acknowledging the role of sexual competition in our evolution as the cause of our enslavement. As animals, our progress is shaped by the need to compete for reproductive success, driving us to survive and adapt. This struggle for sexual dominance not only motivates our evolution but also shapes the fabric of civilization, it's responsible for wars, fashion, art and almost everything we do.

A deterministic reality driven by sexual competition clearly points to a history of enslavement to desire and circumstance. Life produces a deterministic chain of events that enslaves us, this must be recognized before we can hope to be free.

Attempting to persuade a sixteen-year-old boy to suppress his sexual motivations would be both futile and misguided. We need to recognize that these motivations can be harmful; however, society often glorifies and encourages them, which only exacerbates the issue. Our behaviors are influenced by the desires we mimic or emulate, and if we become less preoccupied with sex and love, it would reduce the impact of this condition on human suffering.

> "I wish that people who are conventionally supposed to love each other would say to each other, when they fight, "Please - a little less love, and a little more common decency."
> Kurt Vonnegut, Slapstick

Human biology will not change, we will remain sexually motivated, what can change is an awareness of the fact, and with that a recognition of both the absurdity and enslavement to desire. This awareness will force us to see love as an "infinite pity" instead of the sexual motivation it has always been. This will give us a deep concern for the tragic plight of the other and spur our impulse to engineer methods which will prevent future suffering.

In order to build a religion and society that is functional, we first need individuals who understand these two key principles, 1. that reality is deterministic, and 2. we are driven by sexual motivation.

Then with individuals who seek the truth, and are reasonable, it would then be possible to build a political-economic framework that would produce a democracy that is direct and transparent. To achieve this change, we need a religion that incorporates these two principals, and preaches a belief and law based on them.

THE CHURCH – A DEMOCRACY

A republic is not a democracy, simply electing officials will not produce the ideas we would hope for. An Ekklesia is a Greek word we translate into Church and is the word for the principal assembly of the Greek democracy. For this religion, the Church is where the elect come to govern the kingdom of God. Democracy may work well where a small group of individuals directly choose what they will do collectively, but in larger communities elected officials can, and will be corrupted.

It is fundamental to our current belief that we are all sinners! If there is one thing sinners do, it is to hide their sins, and we know that corruption, or crimes do not fare well when caught in the act. We know criminals and corruption are made dysfunctional by transparency; therefore a transparent economic system is essential.

Simply place the Church online, make it open and transparent, involved in day-to-day commerce, and directly governed by reasonable well-educated people.

An Ekklesia governed by reasonable individuals that understand that reality is deterministic, and driven by sexual dominance, would better recognize the issues in society, and work to correct flawed situations.

With an online, open, transparent, direct democratic framework we would eliminate the church and steeple, and permit individuals to build a political and economic reality providing greater freedom and equality for its adherents.

That would deal with both the Church and the economy, no longer would anyone need to give money to their Church, and the Church would become a primary economic institution within a community, providing education, infrastructure and social services.

The words of Christ are similar to those offered by Socrates, with the added belief that it comes from God's incarnation. If the words of Socrates are enough to get him killed, the words of Christ are far more dangerous to those in power. When power comes from the subjugation of a population, a plan to set people free, could be misinterpreted by the status quo.

This concept I propose should not have any opposition, it is not communism, and can only exist within a free market economy. It does not take over governments, as it is basically a small business run by a Church that promotes education and charity, which is run by its parishioners for the benefit of all.

Furthermore, this community, aside from a few guiding principles, is free to believe as it wishes. This faith does not discriminate: you may be atheist, Jewish, Muslim, or anything else. Perhaps there cannot be two truths, but there can be one underlying truth expressed through many beliefs. Church, then, is where we come to practice diversity and build community.

The goal is to approach the truth, to understand what defines "good" and find your personal spiritual sense. Although the truth is absolute, your belief is your own. Your abilities and actions are what really matter.

THE TRINITY

Any description of a religion must have a God, and this is understood through a trinity, not a divine trinity, but a trinity that is used to understand God within us, and around us.

The first part of the trinity is of course God and is the same as understood by both Platonism and Christianity, unknowable.

The object is to know God, yet this can only be done by faith, as anything unknowable cannot be known. We see God as "good" and to know God is about understanding what good is, for the word may be relative for us but must be a distinct form for God.

The second aspect of the Trinity is the Logos, the Son, the word of God, or Nous, representing intelligence. This can be found through the Church in open and truthful discussions with others, and it can emerge from sources like the Bible, philosophy, science, or any other facet of human knowledge. The Logos is the word of God and can be very effective, but it remains speculative and can never become dogma, as God is ultimately unknowable.

The Holy Spirit is the third aspect of the trinity. This is God's inspiration upon us, upon our Soul, our means to comprehend God's intentions, thus allowing us to align ourselves with God. Consider the Platonic-Christian perspective of a God beyond human understanding, where intelligence is a divine emanation, representing the truth of goodness. The sole path to God is through our capacity to reason, and reason is viewed as the means by which we uncover the truth, or Logos, with the proper development of our Soul being contingent on our quest for truth. Through the development of our Soul and through the Holy Spirit, we work for an individual pursuit of truth and wisdom, whereby we achieve freedom.

According to this view, the ideal community described by Christ depends on our ability to nurture our Souls and to know and comprehend God through the Logos, which the Platonists refer to as intelligence. Religion, in this context, becomes a personal quest to transcend worldly desires, aiming for cognitive and reasoned existence. A society, democracy, or economy cannot be humane or harmonious when its members are seen as mere instinct-driven beings, lacking in soul and engaging in base sexual competition.

Therefore, since Christ suffered in his body, arm yourselves also with the same attitude, because whoever suffers in the body is done with sin. As a result, they do not live the rest of their earthly lives for evil human desires, but rather for the will of God. 1 Peter 4

Although seemingly simple and straightforward with just two principles and a trinity, this concept is actually quite radical. If God is the Unknown cause, causality suggests that human behavior cannot be merely explained by free will. Instead, it is influenced by either the first cause, the absence of it, or the human modification of it. While the origin or creator is unknowable, we can understand certain aspects with some certainty. However, as Wittgenstein argued, there are limits to what we can discuss seriously, this forces us to have faith in order to understand the many aspects of reality that are beyond our understanding.

The second principle emphasizes our sexual motivations, revealing that we are often enslaved by our desires. Through a clearer understanding of this principle, we achieve not only greater personal freedom but also a natural decrease in the transgressions that impact our fellow human beings.

Please let me restate these principles:

1. There is no free will, therefore we must forgive all transgressors, and work to repair the world, what a Kabbalist would call "Tikkum Olahm."

2. We are motivated through sexual competition, which enslaves us and produces irrational behavior. Once we know this, we no longer take seriously the many pointless motivations we have.

The goal of religion is to draw us closer to God; to do this, each of us must first define a true Logos. The path to God requires us to apply this Logos to guide our soul's evolution. Through this maturity, we learn to relinquish material desires, fortify our pursuit of truth, broaden our compassion for life, gain a true awareness of our reality, and arrive at a serene acceptance of death.

9. Platonism to Christianity: The Evolution of Divine Reason

A first-century Platonist would have understood the logos as the universal reason or principle that orders the cosmos and provides coherence. The concept of the logos was not introduced by Christianity but by Heraclitus, a pre-Socratic Greek philosopher who lived around 500 BC. He was born in Ephesus, the same city where the Apostle Paul would later teach Christianity. He used the term to describe the underlying order and rationality of the universe.

For Platonist's, the logos was seen as the divine reason that permeates all things and connects the material world with the metaphysical realm of forms or ideas.

The Greek Platonic concepts of both the Trinity and the Logos were modified and then incorporated into the new Christian faith for the first century Roman Empire.

For first-century Christians, the "Logos" and the "Word of God" were synonymous; Jesus Christ is the Logos, both are one and the same. These terms describe the Nous or Intelligence, which is the second aspect of the Platonic Trinity, the only aspect of God we can know.

> *"In the beginning was the Word (Logos), and the Logos was with God, and the Logos was God." — John 1:1*

> *"The Word became flesh and made his dwelling among us. We have seen his glory, the glory of the one and only Son, who came from the Father, full of grace and truth." — John 1:14*

In this reinterpretation of the Genesis story, Jesus Christ is identified as the Word (Logos), existing with God from the beginning and being one with God. "Logos," originally a Greek term, meaning "reason," "discourse," or "principle."

Particularly within Stoicism, Logos referred to the divine, animating principle of the universe, a concept foundational to Greek philosophy, and is not in any way part of Jewish tradition.

The concept of the Trinity also draws from Platonic ideas. While Plato did not describe a Trinity, the Platonic framework includes the One (the Good), the Intellect (Nous), and the Soul (Psyche), forming a metaphysical triad. In a Christian context, the "One" aligns with the unknowable God, the Intellect (Nous) represents Christ, or the Son, and instead of the Soul, Christians hold that the third element, the Holy Spirit, is a divine force that guides the Soul toward good, or God.

Thus, within this view, Logos (as Christ) represents divine intellect, the second aspect of the Trinity, with God as the unknowable One, the first aspect. The third aspect, the Holy Spirit, acts upon the human soul, guiding it toward God or ultimate goodness.

To be able to understand the relationship between Platonism and Christianity, it is important to understand the Platonic concept of Forms, which was central to Plato's philosophy.

Similar to how Christians understand God's connection to Angels, in Plato's view, Forms are the perfect, unchanging concepts or ideals that exist in an abstract realm (heaven), beyond our physical world. Everything we see in the physical world is just an imperfect reflection or copy of these perfect Forms. For example, when we see a beautiful object, it is beautiful because it participates in the Form of Beauty, which is perfect and unchanging. The Platonic form of beauty is not that which is in the eye of the beholder, it is an ideal and perfect beauty, something that requires maturity of the soul to see. It is very possible to see something as beautiful that is not beautiful, or think someone is wise that is not. The Forms are close to God, perfection, and therefor almost unknowable.

The central value of Christianity lies in Christ as the Logos, the divine principle of reason and truth. In this sense, God, or what we call the "Good," is understood as a Platonic form, the highest and most difficult to grasp. We approach this truth not through ritual or temple, but through the maturation of the soul, guided by the Holy Spirit. Christianity, at its heart, is a deeply personal and lifelong effort toward intelligence, self-realization, and the cultivation of wisdom. The path to God is the path of soul-making: to live authentically, to grow in understanding, and to prepare ourselves for death.

These are some key points to understand about Platonic Forms:

1. Forms are perfect examples of concepts or qualities (e.g., Beauty, Justice, Equality).
2. Forms do not change; they are eternal and constant.

3. Forms exist independently of the objects in the physical world.
4. Forms are universal; the Form of Beauty, for instance, applies to all beautiful things.

Plato believed that true knowledge is knowledge of these Forms. While we can only perceive the physical world through our senses, we can grasp the Forms through our intellect and reasoning. The same should be said about the Christian Logos, we can grasp the Logos or Christ through our intellect and reasoning.

Philo of Alexandria (20 BC– 50 CE), also called Philo Judaeus, was a Hellenistic Jewish philosopher who lived in Alexandria, in the Roman province of Egypt. He gives us an insight into how important Hellenism and the Philosophy of Platonism was to many Jews at the time of Christ. Philo interprets the Logos, which is the Divine Mind as a Platonic Form of Forms, the Idea of Ideas or the sum total of Forms or Ideas. The Logos is an indestructible Form of wisdom, also known as Sophia.

The Apostle Paul must have also seen the Platonic similarities to the Trinity, their Unknowable God, and Soul, all of which are not part of his Jewish faith.

Comparisons between Christianity and Platonism:
1. **Dualism**: The New Testament often contrasts the earthly realm with the heavenly or spiritual realm, suggesting a dualistic view similar to Platonism .

2. **The Soul:** Both see the soul as eternal and existing independently of the body.

3. **Idea of the Good:** Of God as the ultimate source of goodness and light in the New Testament is parallel to Plato's Idea of the Good.

4. **Knowledge and Wisdom**: Both Plato and the New Testament emphasize the importance of knowledge and wisdom.

Modern scholarly consensus holds that the Torah makes no reference to an immortal soul independent of the body. The Trinity and its Logos is absolutely a Platonic concept, and the reason why the Virgin Mary and Sophia are such common names for many Catholic institutions.

Christianity is the Ekklēsia, originally the principal assembly of ancient Athens during its Golden Age, the time of the world's first democracy, and the only polis until the United States became a government resembling a democracy.

I do not believe Christ ever intended for His church to become a tool for domination used to control a population. The Church of Christ was to be a spiritual and political governing body, a lawful assembly of free people, a force that made the Logos of God a spiritual reality on the material earth. We know this because the Greek word Ekklesia, used for Church by Jesus, was a political term, used in the government of the assemblies of those days.

It is only through our Soul that we can know Christ, the Word, Logos, Nous, Intelligence, Will to Life, or Divine Mind.... call it what you will, but it is only through our Soul that Christians can know the "Word of Christ." Our Soul is not born "intelligent," it must be developed from our discovery of "truth," which in turn comes from our ability to "reason." Therefore, in order to have a Soul that is of any value, we each must be able to reason, and discover the truth, and this is why Christ says...

"But the Advocate, the Holy Spirit, whom the Father will send in my name, will teach you all things and will remind you of everything I have said to you." John 14:26

The Church, or Ekklēsia, is the place where Christ, the "Logos," or "reasoned discourse" should take place. We are all sinners, but not so much when others are present, Church is how a community finds the truth, through a transparent dialogue about how to understand the Logos, how to behave, and what work must be done for Christ.

"Truly, truly, I say to you, whoever believes in me will also do the works that I do; and greater works than these will he do, because I am going to the Father." John 14:12

Life is a task to be done, first to mature the soul through the understanding of what is good, then to act accordingly. The governing body of the Christian community is not a Church or Synagogue filled with ceremony, or rants and singing, but a reasoned discussion on how to govern, and as such would have built the community spoken of, and hoped for by Christ in the New Testament.

Today western theology is a dual search for redemption, one of the New Testament for the Gentiles and another for the Jews found in the Old Testament. Between the master and slave, the goy and chosen, a theology was molded into a religion from our animal characteristics of sexual dominance.

Our modern economic system offers more than enough potential to fulfill both the Jewish, Islamic and Christian view of redemption, where there is no longer any need for a slave class to till the fields, nor any benefit gained from a master class to exist from the toil of others. The meek can and should inherit the earth, the chosen people can return to Israel, and the Christians can love their neighbors, and we can make all this happen without further human conflict.

There is such an excess of material things in the developed world that it's only a matter of time before we reject the material in favor of the aesthetic. Education is what turns our attention to more aesthetic and selfless goals. Education must become our new status marker, what we evangelize must be truth and knowledge, then the working class will produce art, the priest class will educate and govern us, all while the leisure class will become stylistically absurd.

The truth has always been kept away from as many as possible, secret societies, inquisitions, and outlawed books have been the norm. Belief is controlled... but today information is close at hand to anyone, giving us the ability to dramatically improve our consciousness, as well as the practical aspects of living.

We are responsible to be honest and careful in how we define the truth, we are the jurors of our reality.

With a true understanding of who we are, our lives will be enriched with love and peace. Today, for once in all history, we can actually act to produce utopia and end this absurdity.

In order for this to take place, for this Utopia, or Messianic age to become real, we simply need to know what to do, and do it. Unfortunately, although simple, we are so far from the mark, that this will be a radical change of belief from the current status quo.

Platonic forms are those ideals imagined that we then make real, we build things that were once metaphysical and make them part of reality. We discovered America, we discovered electricity, we discovered computers, all these things were there and were not created by us, but were already there when we came to them. Technology is given to us by God, it is a Platonic form, we discover it and evolve from it because we search for truth. Reading and writing is also a technology, and by definition the word.

If Christianity is a set of instructions to save the meek, humble and oppressed, then it has failed, yet there is a set of words which form a Logos which actually works, and it is this new Logos that will be transformative to us.

I have compared religion to an algorithm, and know that there are instructions for a better world, we can find these instructions in the same way we find Christ, because the knowledge is within us.

Today's technology will educate us, feed us, and provide a collaborative way for Churches, Synagogues, Mosques, and communities to manage themselves. Transparency will weed out the hypocrites and bad actors, compelling congregations and businesses to compete not for profit, but to do real honest good.

When we abandon the absurdity of good and evil, and the mistaken concept of Satan, we will see that evil is no more than primitive human behavior patterns which arise from our sexual nature, and lack of education. We will fear stupidity and pity our transgressors. We must see that we are not that far removed from a chimp, that evil is left behind when we evolve from the flesh, to the spirit, rather from animal to well educated humans.

10. Kabbalah - Tikkun Olam and the Path Forward

The Kabbalistic tradition, especially as it evolved through the later Sabbatean and Frankist movements, was instrumental in popularizing the idea of a strict cosmic dualism of good and evil within Western thought. This shift heightened the apocalyptic dimensions of Jewish eschatology, framing history as a drama that would culminate in a final messianic confrontation, a structure strikingly similar to the Christian vision of Revelation.

This was no small departure. The Hebrew Bible presents a sovereign God who governs all aspects of life, adversity included, without positing a rival cosmic force. Yet, under the influence of these Kabbalistic currents, a new emphasis emerged: history as a stage for ultimate conflict, resolved only in a definitive Messianic Age. In this way, Jewish eschatology absorbed a framework of dualistic struggle that had once been more at home in Christian theology.

Today, Judaism is largely shaped by Kabbalistic thought, though this was not always the case. Much like Christianity absorbed and reconfigured elements from the diverse religions of the Roman world, Kabbalah drew upon earlier traditions and philosophies, particularly Platonic concepts, and anchored them to the opening chapter of Ezekiel. His vision of the divine "chariot" (Merkavah) became the foundational image of Jewish mysticism.

The parallels to Platonism are striking. The Platonic "One" (good), Neoplatonism's Monad, and the Kabbalistic *Ein Sof* all are abstract, transcendent concepts for a divine ultimate reality that is beyond comprehension and the source of all existence.

Each tradition wrestles with the same question: how can an infinite, unbounded reality give rise to a finite and fractured world?

Though debated among scholars, it is clear that both Christian mysticism and Jewish Kabbalah reflect the deep imprint of Platonic and later Neo-Platonism thought, reframing its metaphysical vision within their own religious frameworks.

Kabbalah, emerging in 12th-century Spain, became a bridge between esoteric Jewish and Christian circles, offering a mystical framework through which concepts akin to the Book of Revelation could be understood and operationalized. It translated the evolving Platonic worldview into Jewish mystical language, ultimately casting the Jewish pursuit as redemption through sin, contrasting with Christianity's emphasis on redemption through righteousness.

The earliest known proto-Kabbalistic text, the *Sefer Yetzirah*, dates to the Second Century. Attributed either to Abraham or to Rabbi Akiva, although modern scholarship considers it an anonymous composition composed between the 3rd and 6th centuries CE.

The *Zohar*, now central to Jewish Kabbalah, appeared in Spain in the late 13th century, composed by Moses de León, though traditionally attributed to the 2nd-century sage Rabbi Shimon bar Yochai. Linguistic analysis, historical inconsistencies, and accounts from de León's widow suggest he was the principal author, motivated as much by profit as by piety.

The *Zohar* gained particular prominence following the expulsion of Jews from Spain in 1492. By the 16th century, exiled Jews in Safed, Israel, had established the "Safed School of Kabbalah." Visionaries like Isaac Luria and Yosef Caro developed new mystical ideas that profoundly shaped Jewish practice and thought, cementing Safed's reputation as the "City of Kabbalah." The Lurianic Kabbalah introduced concepts such as the dual pillars of Mercy (*Chesed*) and Severity (*Gevurah*), inadvertently importing a moral dualism reminiscent of Zoroastrian cosmology. It was from this milieu that Shabbatai Zevi emerged, advocating a radical Messianic theology of "redemption through sin," where acts previously deemed sinful were reframed as righteous within his Messianic vision.

If the analysis of this book is correct, the theological structure of Mithraism forms a hidden backbone of Catholicism, promoting a cosmic conflict between good and evil alongside a celestial end-times narrative drawn from Zoroastrian thought. It is not inconceivable that the Messianic fervor surrounding Shabbatai Zevi was, in some sense, encouraged or utilized by the Church to advance this shared eschatological vision.

Sabbatai Zevi's father, Mordecai, held a position of influence as a local agent for prominent English and Dutch trading houses, a role that brought both wealth and social standing. Sabbatai's connections to England, combined with the turbulent political and social currents of his era, raise the intriguing possibility that his proclaimed Messianic Age was not purely mystical but at least partially orchestrated, a maneuver shaped by political interests. In this view, messianism becomes more than theology; it becomes a tool, wielded to direct populations, consolidate influence, and align

Jewish and European power networks under carefully managed religious symbolism.

I will not explore this entire history here, this book is concerned with the story from Creation to Christ, but a few key dates and events will help illuminate how, after the expulsion of the Jews from Spain in 1492 and the Protestant Reformation of 1517, strange new alliances began to form. Both the expelled Jewish communities and the emerging Protestant states found a common adversary in the Catholic Church. History shows a simple truth: when people are oppressed, they begin to organize against their oppressors.

In 1540, the Jesuit Order was established by papal approval under St. Ignatius of Loyola to defend and expand Catholic power. By contrast, the first Masonic lodges, whose roots many link to esoteric Kabbalistic ideas, appear in Scotland by 1599.

Soon the English Civil Wars (1642–1651) will paved the way for Oliver Cromwell's rule. In 1656, Menasseh ben Israel, a rabbi and Kabbalist who had fled Catholic persecution in Portugal, traveled to England to petition Cromwell for the readmission of Jews. A man of strong millenarian conviction, Menasseh found common cause with English Christian millenarians, whose support strengthened his appeal. Through his efforts, Jews were formally readmitted to England after centuries of exile.

The Catholic Church, sensing the rise of secret networks, issued its first ban on Freemasonry in 1738, and various monarchs expelled the Jesuits starting in the 1750s, with Portugal leading the way.

These events formed the backdrop to a deeper transformation. In Protestant England, Catholic worship was illegal from 1559 until well after the American Revolution. At the same time, Kabbalah, evolving through its Sabbatean currents, was quietly influencing not only Jewish communities but also esoteric strands of Protestantism. Both Jews and Protestants, facing Catholic domination, were drawn to a mystical framework that promised hidden knowledge and power. Yet this was not something to be preached openly; Kabbalah for both Jew and Christian remained a secret discipline.

From these converging streams arose a nascent network of ideas and societies, Freemasonry foremost among them, that blended Protestant, Jewish, and even Catholic elements under the banner of secrecy. Over time this produced a subtle theological shift. Christianity began to adopt the "older brother" view of Judaism, elevating Jewish choseness as part of its own self-understanding. This Sabbatean influence, though rarely named, still echoes in the modern world: consider the fervent Christian support for policies in Israel, even for actions like the Gaza genocide, or the way powerful networks of influence, such as those surrounding figures like Jeffrey Epstein, seem to thrive on secrecy and the manipulation of moral boundaries. Evil, after all, can be an effective tool in the pursuit of power, so long as it remains hidden.

Religion has always been a story written to control, a tool wielded by priests, leaders, and secret societies. Today, the powerful study Platonism and Kabbalah, the frameworks that have long guided thought and authority. But the time has come to turn these tools toward liberation, not domination.

For centuries, the Jewish people were slowly cast as "chosen" under Sabbatean doctrine, seeking redemption through sin. This absurdity must end. The ultimate Jewish calling today must be to redefine the Messianic Age itself. It is a call to collective action: to embody the principle of Mashiach through Tikkun Olam, repairing the world and leading humanity not with a single savior, but through our shared responsibility. Christians and Muslims, guided by principles of compassion and service, will naturally join in. If the Jewish people do not lead, reason itself demands action; the absurdity of our world must not continue.

History suggests that the Israelites first served as a defensive outpost on Egypt's frontier, and later as Europe's administrators mediating between power and servitude. Today, that legacy must be redirected toward humanity itself. For power to truly serve the people, our future systems of governance, justice, and social order must be transparent, participatory, inclusive, and accountable.

Tikkun Olam cannot be left to secrecy. It must be built on open platforms, decentralized institutions, and systems that respect human diversity. Social media tools and AI can help us educate, monitor, and repair every facet of society, ensuring that truth, fairness, and progress prevail.

This is a call to reason, to collective action, and to moral awakening. Faith, once a weapon of division, can become a force of unity. By embracing logic, reassessing inherited beliefs, and aligning our spiritual understanding with reality, we can transform conflict into cooperation, absurdity into purpose, and division into harmony.

We stand at a crossroads. The time has come to cast aside the old paradigms of division and rise above our base instincts. Look around, have we not amassed enough material wealth? This must be the Messianic Age, no longer a distant hope but a present reality. The question is no longer *if* it will come, but *what we are willing to become* in order to bring it forth.

historyreligionandtruth.com

www.ingramcontent.com/pod-product-compliance
Lightning Source LLC
Chambersburg PA
CBHW060155050426
42446CB00013B/2833